THE ELECTRONIC CRIMINALS

THE ELECTRONIC CRIMINALS

ROBERT FARR

McGraw-Hill Book Company
New York   St. Louis   San Francisco
Düsseldorf   London   Mexico   Sydney   Toronto

123456789BPBP798765

Library of Congress Cataloging in Publication Data

Farr, Robert.
    The electronic criminals.

    1. Commercial crimes. 2. Business intelligence.
3. Crime and criminals. I. Title.
HV6768.F37   364.1'6   74-30231
ISBN 0-07-019962-0

To Betty, my love and my wife,
for her patience and understanding,
and to her parents, Bert and Jane,
with thanks for letting me take her
from them

Preface

All effective criminal activity depends on some measure of illusion. Once that illusion is thoroughly shattered by exposure a particular criminal *modus operandi* can never have quite the same sting.

No point is served by pretending that the fault lies primarily with the criminals and their accomplices. These people are symptoms of a contemporary sickness, not its cause. They use the methods of crime, not necessarily because they are less restrained and less decent nor because they have greater contempt for the law than their ancestors, but because present-day society insists on being "screwed."

Electronic crime affects society in general. More and more people freely admit, indeed positively boast, that they are not loyal to society and do not intend to serve its interests. Such people are potential supercriminals.

Modern technological thieves are not few in number because their access to the mass media, their attitudes, their social influence, and their philosophy enjoy enormous and permanent attention. Various large, and very significant, groups are interested only in "doing their thing" independently and regardless of each other. What seems virtuous and normal to one group seems vicious and abnormal to another.

But our society is still deeply moral. As electronic criminals pile their swag as high as Mount Everest without society apparently raising a finger, as government officials lie and cheat and steal to stay in power with society apparently accepting the doctrine that "might makes right," and as TV commercials "take in" millions of consumers who rush out to the shops to buy dreams spun off an electronic screen, society appears to be in a state of moral inertia. But beneath our social permissiveness our conscience runs strong.

Our world is still a fine place in which to live—a better one perhaps than any previous generation has enjoyed. But some of the people in it are causing serious problems. In 1974 many people experienced diminishing respect for persons in high places who acted as if they were above the law, and this led to a loss of respect for the concept of leadership itself. We should not confuse diminishing respect for a president with respect for the presidency, for example. Our society needs people in high places. It cannot function without leadership at every level, from the head of a household to the manager of a business to a chief of state.

What is missing in our society today is the necessary preparation and training for the responsibilities of authority in high places. If parents in the home and people in business and government never learned the lessons of fair play when they were growing up, we cannot expect them to know how to play fair when they reach high places. Consequently we all suffer every time "the boss" makes expedient judgments rather than proper moral decisions.

If coming generations are to be spared the tragic consequences of even more widespread corruption, the teaching of morality in the family and in the school ought to be as important to us as curbing inflation and other socioeconomic problems. Our children should be taught how to deal with everyday actions fairly and ethically. They should be exposed to those philosophical and ethical concepts, with practical examples that illustrate the alternatives of right and wrong so that they are better able to cope.

Robert Farr
Roquebrune-Cap-Martin
August 1974

Contents

1

Conned
by the
Computer Criminal

What financial experience could the following people possibly have shared during the early summer of 1974?

Jack Benny, comedian	$300,000
David Cassidy, rock singer	$300,000
Liza Minnelli, actress and entertainer	$231,000
Andy Williams, singer	$538,000
Walter Matthau, actor	$200,000
Fred Borch, ex-chairman of General Electric	$440,920
Russell McFall, chairman and president of Western Union	$394,000
Walter Wriston, chairman of First National City Bank of New York	$211,000
Earl Kinter, Washington lawyer	$127,000
Henry Fox, Washington lawyer	$108,000
Ralph Hart, director of Heublein Company	$322,000

All of them joined the Victims, a not-so-exclusive club whose members suffer as much as the victims of muggings, although they may not have the visible scars to prove it. The numbers in the right-hand column indicate how much money each of the Victims lost. Some could better afford the loss than others but few of them will ever recover from the humiliation.

Their money was stolen with the help of a computer. Each one of these victims still feels it should never have happened. They believed firmly in the integrity of the computer.

But it did happen. What is surprising is that many of these victims are economically sophisticated and should know that computers are as honest or as dishonest as the people who feed information into them. One would hope that senior corporate executives, professional investors, lawyers and heads of international banks would be harder to swindle than a housewife like Mrs. Louise Jones, for example.

Mrs. Jones visited the local shopping center near her Cincinnati, Ohio, home. She made purchases in several shops and paid by check for every one over two dollars. Each time, she presented her bank check card to the clerk to identify herself and guarantee that the check would be honored. Mrs. Jones was completely unaware that a man had been watching her every move. When she wheeled her shopping cart into the parking lot, the man followed her.

"I was chatting with a neighbor on the way to my car when this man came up and accused me of passing a phony check in Woolworth's," Mrs. Jones told the Better Business Bureau investigators. "I was terribly embarrassed. I had paid by check in Woolworth's, and I knew there was money in the bank to cover it. But having him say that it was bogus in front of my friend just confused the life out of me. I was tongue-tied."

The man had been convincing. When he accosted her, he said politely, "We've had a negative report on your bank check card from the computer."

The use of the word computer was the key. It instantly

implied that an infallible machine had caught Mrs. Jones in a misdeed.

"Let me have your bank card and checkbook, please," the man said next, "and enough cash to cover the check you gave Woolworth's. This will show your good faith, madam. Perhaps I can clear up the matter for you."

"I only wanted to stop him talking. People were all around and looking at me and I was almost in tears," Mrs. Jones said. "I gave him my documents and five dollars. He told me to stay where I was until he returned."

Mrs. Jones and her friend waited in the parking lot nearly half an hour. Then the girl suggested that something must be wrong and they ought to go to Woolworth's.

Of course, no one in the store knew anything about her checkbook or bank card. The store manager, who was familiar with this kind of swindle, told her to telephone her bank and the police. He invited Mrs. Jones to use the telephone in his office. By the time she reported the matter to her bank, $170 worth of goods had been bought by the man and his accomplices with her checks.

"I didn't lose the money personally," Mrs. Jones said sadly. "My bank covered the loss because I informed them immediately. But I was so upset by being conned that I had nightmares about it for more than a month."

The French traffic warden, Jacqueline Faure, was victimized twice in the same day by a computer criminal using similar methods. Like Mrs. Jones, she had turned over her documents to a man in a shopping center. When he did not return, she became suspicious and went to the shop he pretended to represent. Once she realized that she had been conned and had reported the matter to her bank and to the Gendarmerie, Mlle. Faure returned home. She then received a phone call from a man who claimed to be the manager of the shop.

"We've found your checkbook and bank card," he told her. "The thief probably was frightened and threw them into a trash can. Can you come to my office at once and claim them?"

When she got to the shop, the perplexed manager

assured her that he had not made a telephone call to her home, and certainly did not have her documents.

Realizing what had happened, Mlle. Faure took a taxi back to her apartment, but arrived too late. The man who had made the bogus call—her home telephone number was in the documents he took from her—had already broken in and ransacked her rooms. From the notes she had written on the stubs of her checkbook he learned that she had recently bought a portable TV, sterling silver candlesticks and several other items of value. All were gone. The thief left behind this note: "Thank you, mademoiselle—double thanks."

Although losses in the cases of Mrs. Jones and Mlle. Faure total less than $500, the two women were no less victimized than the prominent people who make up the rest of our list. In proportion to their savings and income their losses from being duped were just as great. Bank and insurance executives in the United Kingdom suggest that 2,000 cases of checkbook and bank card swindles occur each month in the British Isles. Statistics on such swindles in the United States and other countries are difficult to compile, but one New York bank acknowledges that it made good $1,270,000 worth of checks written by thieves on the accounts of its depositors in 1973. Most of these checks were accepted on presentation of stolen bank guarantee identity cards, controlled by computers.

On June 26, 1974, the *Wall Street Journal* referred to the swindle that fooled the eleven prominent people listed as possibly the biggest of its kind in history. It was based on the classic Ponzi scheme, named for Charles Ponzi, who in 1919 and 1920 promised investors $1.40 in ninety days for every $1 invested. He paid off early investors with money from more recent investors and took in $10 million before his arrest, conviction and imprisonment.

The 1974 version was an oil-drilling scheme that used the computer merely as window dressing. In 1955, the promoters began raising money for drilling oil wells.

They persuaded several well-known persons to invest and made certain that they received prompt and generous returns on their money, although the company drilled only a few dry 500-foot holes and one legitimate 3,500-foot well. Then the promoters attracted others by mentioning the prominent people who had put money into the venture. Few investors exercised enough care to check on the operations.

One victim, a banker, said, "I take a harder look at the background of a man who comes in for a loan to buy a new car than I did at the oil drilling company. I just telephoned a Hollywood star whose films we have financed and asked him what he thought of the deal. He said that he had put in $100,000 and got back $155,000 in less than six months. So I sent him my check for over $200,000, only I have yet to see any returns. All I have for my money is about fifty pounds of computer print-outs supposedly describing the operations."

To make the offer more impressive to prospective investors, the company programmed a computer to generate hundreds of sheets of data allegedly describing in depth the productivity of wells on a California vegetable farm, where irrigation pipes had been painted orange and marked with oil-field codes. From photographs of the layout it is impossible to tell that only water runs in those pipes, not the oil reported by the computer.

In September 1973, the Securities and Exchange Commission called it a "Ponzi scheme" and declared the oil drilling company insolvent. Four groups of victims have filed lawsuits in federal courts accusing the principals in the oil-drilling company of wrongdoing. Investors had sunk almost $130 million in the swindle before the company was forced into bankruptcy; all but $30 million has vanished. By bringing suits, the investors hope to recover a few cents on the dollar of their investments and to justify tax deductions for some of the balance of their losses.

Another recent multimillion swindle involving computer fraud was the Equity Funding case. In March 1973,

Raymond L. Dirks, an unconventional stockbroker with a wide following on Wall Street, received a tip from a disgruntled former employee of the Equity Funding Corporation of America that sent him on a tense, investigative odyssey without precedent in the history of finance. It was a trail of fraud, forgery, intimidation, conspiracy, and, above all, computer crime.

The Equity Funding hoax is the most monumental money swindle of modern times. Through a spectacular scheme of fakery, Equity Funding had created over $100 million in fictitious assets. It had forged death certificates, counterfeited bonds, and created bogus insurance policies. Equity Funding fooled everyone—investment advisors, banks, lawyers, accountants, auditors, insurance examiners, the Securities and Exchange Commission, the system that buttressed it, the stockholders who bought it.

The Equity Funding case involves millions of hijacked dollars, fraudulent records, and doctored tapes. Computer print-outs concealed the massive fraud and fakery. Tapes were programmed so that computers would reject incriminating data and accept and produce only what would support the conspiracy. Computers were also used in playing hide-and-seek with investigators by switching data damaging to the swindlers from one code to another, just a step ahead of the authorities.

After the Equity scandal was exposed, several Equity investors decided to sue IBM for $4 billion, claiming that the company's inability to manufacture a swindle-proof computer had contributed to their loss. Despite the fact that IBM had claimed their computers are virtually tamper proof, the case was thrown out of court. Obviously no one can be expected to be perfect, not even an IBM computer.

The villains in these incidents took the hard way to swindle their victims. If they had actually employed the computer as a tool they could have laid hands on millions of dollars' worth of negotiable securities without launching a big promotion, and indeed without leaving the comfort and safety of their own homes. The money is as near as a telephone and a teleprinter machine.

We are living in a certificateless society; signed and sealed stock and bond certificates are no longer the basis for establishing the ownership of many securities. Those beautifully engraved certificates have been replaced by computer print-outs to almost the same extent as credit cards have taken the place of cash and checks.

To lay hands on big wealth, the villain need only obtain a push-button telephone (new from manufacturers or second-hand in shops) and a teleprinter (which can be leased or bought second-hand). In many countries the telephone company will install this equipment for a nominal fee, or, with the guidance of an installation manual from a bookstore, he can do it himself. Hooking up such equipment to telephone lines requires no special tools or skills, provided the lines are capable of handling such services—as they are in most Western countries except certain exchanges in Great Britain and France.

The next step requires some ingenuity. A computer memory bank that serves as a depository for shares of stocks and other negotiable securities must be located. This can be done in several ways. The villain can take a job at a computer center which services investment firms, or he can bribe someone who already works in such a place to supply copies of computer print-outs that list the securities on hand. The villain must also learn the code number that unlocks the computer's memory bank and gives access to its processing facilities from a remote station (telephone or teleprinter).

Once supplied with this information and the hardware in his home, the villain merely has to put in a call to the computer. This can be done from a distance of hundreds of miles or even from a foreign country. The computer will follow, without any interference, the instructions given over the telephone. Within seconds after the villain communicates his order to the computer, his teleprinter will begin to type out a confirmation document transferring the securities from the designated portfolio into his hands. In time—possibly a very long time—the theft will be discovered but by then the villain will have had time to sell the stolen shares—and a buyer will have had time to resell them, and so on with the original theft becoming lost in a chain of transactions.

It is accepted as normal that securities "get lost" for a time in computer files. Nobody worries greatly about it; it is assumed that they will turn up when the computer sorts itself out. The Borden Company once "lost" part of its investment portfolio through a computer error and was not aware of the loss until more than two years later.

The criminal method described above is not simply theoretical. A man named Manfred Stein was accused of successfully operating such an electronic stock swindle from his bedside telephone and teleprinter. Had it not been for an unfortunate coincidence, this might have escaped undetected. Allegedly, after receiving confirmation that the stocks had been transferred to his possession, Stein instructed the computer to erase all records of the transactions. However, unbeknown to him, telephone company engineers had monitored his lines during a routine check on the quality of service. They became suspicious and reported the strange communications to police. Investigators called on Stein and asked questions that alarmed him. Later, when they returned with a warrant for his arrest on the charge of using public telephone services for illegal transactions, they discovered he had fled, taking the telephone and teleprinter with him. A week earlier, one broker claimed he had paid Stein $300,000 for several blocks of stocks which were stolen. Warrants for Stein's arrest are still outstanding. It is believed that he is living comfortably under an alias on an island in the Caribbean.

There are $8 billion worth of negotiable securities stored in a single computer in New York City today, according to the August 1973 report of the U.S. Senate Permanent Subcommittee on Investigations. They are just waiting for some electronic criminal to gain access to the computer and tell it where to send the stocks and bonds. Wouldn't almost anyone be tempted if he thought he would never be caught, or that, if caught, the only punishment would be a rap on the wrist?

It's exciting to toy with the idea of becoming a millionaire just by pushing the right buttons. During a recent conference on data processing in Hamburg, I sat in on a late evening discussion with a group of computer experts who were exposing some existing weaknesses in computer security by theoretically robbing banks, security firms and government agencies of millions of dollars through their computers. It was good fun, and purely academic. After "robbing" the Fort Knox computer, they drank a nightcap and went off to their hotel rooms. But not so amusing is a study by the Stanford Research Institute which revealed that in the five-year period ending in 1972 some 50,000 major crimes were committed worldwide with the assistance of such products of modern technology as computers, telecommunications devices, photocopy equipment, lasers, jet air transportation and so on. Since only one in four persons who commit such crimes is ever apprehended, the actual figure for technology-assisted crime in that period is probably nearer 200,000.

The Stanford study details what kinds of people become technology-assisted thieves. Few of them were found to have had prior criminal records. In many cases they are respected citizens who simply have been given sufficient motivation and the means to do wrong. Among the reasons why they turn to crime are: to get back at an employer; to try to be "somebody"; to get what the world "owes" them before it is too late; to get out of personal financial difficulties; and prove themselves superior to those "damn computers." Many had access to inside information on how to gain possession of property belonging to an employer or customer. Some of them held positions of trust and had resisted temptations for years, until one day when the motivation became too great and they betrayed the trust.

When we add these people to the numbers of professional crooks, con men and other kinds of criminals who practice their trade with the help of modern technology, we begin to realize that we are becoming increasingly vulnerable to fraud, theft, forgery, embezzlement, extortion, sabotage and other crimes. This state of affairs is an undesirable fringe benefit of the extraordinary growth of technology in our times.

The idea of an international crime-fighting force was first proposed in 1914, by Prince Albert I of Monaco, whose concern was prevention and control of crime committed in and against his famous gambling casino. It was not until 1946, however, that his concept, in the form of Interpol, was realized, and even that agency has not become the worldwide police force he envisioned. In 1973, twenty-seven years after its founding, police officials from 114 nations met in Vienna to discuss ways and means to provide a daily exchange of intelligence about the movements of frontier-jumping crooks. But little more was accomplished than an affirmation that this was a good idea.

The main obstacle to effective international law enforcement is the jungle of extradition laws that exists throughout the world, and the lowering of barricades between countries. At the present time, it is possible for electronic criminals to move freely from country to country even when they are running from the law. Goods can also be profitably transported across the virtually open borders. In May 1974, a British firm was convicted of more than sixty-five counts of illegal trade in butter. The firm legally exported butter from Belgium to Britain. The firm then sent allegedly empty trucks back to Belgium. In fact, the trucks were filled with the same butter, which was sold at a profit of over $6,000 per seven-ton load. The butter on its export from Belgium had received about $900 per ton in subsidy from Common Market farm funds. When it was reimported into Belgium and sold on the open market it realized a $900 profit per ton. The penalty for illegally turning profits of over $300,000 was a fine of $7,500. The crooks were reportedly very pleased.

Suspects usually cannot be prosecuted for crimes committed in another country (with the exception of such offenses as murder, manslaughter, bigamy and a few others). Roving international criminals are aware of the loopholes and operate accordingly. A thief can use a stolen credit card for several days in one country, buying thousands of dollars' worth of goods and services, before the credit card firm adds the card to its "hot sheet." Then he has only to slip over the border into another country—perhaps using a first-class airline ticket bought with the stolen card—and he is beyond the reach of the law. American Express, Diners Club, BankAmericard and other credit cards firms have files bulging with reports of such cases. "Many professionals keep themselves clean in their home country," states Rex Smith, Chief Inspector in Europe for American Express, "so that they will always have a refuge from the law."

What is needed is legislation to allow prosecution in any country of anyone who has perpetrated a crime beyond its frontiers. Plans are now being made to establish an international computer center to process data on the activities of travelling criminals, but the millions of dollars this International Crime Reporting Facility will cost cannot be justified if laws do not exist to punish the offenders.

The real remedy, however, is to be found in prevention and protection. Since the business community suffers more from technological crime than any other group of victims, it seems logical that the problem should be solved in the Board Room.

Long-established business methods breed a false sense of security which provides absolutely no defense against the clever and determined new international criminal. Many firms rely on registered air mail to send valuable items from one country to another. This is inviting trouble, as the First National City Bank of New York (known as "Citibank") found out early in 1974, when it was the victim of a $1 million theft, probably the biggest air mail robbery in history.

On Tuesday, January 8, 1974, the New York office of Citibank bundled 1,000 travellers' checks, each worth $1,000, into a postal packet about six inches thick. It was addressed to London headquarters, from which checks were to be distributed to Citibank offices throughout Europe. A customs declaration, listing the contents—advertising might be a better word—was glued to the packet. In due course, the million-dollar package was taken to a post office, where it was registered, stamped and sent off to Kennedy Airport to be included in a sack of mail destined for the next flight to London. The travellers' checks were insured, but not for their full value. From the time the bank consigned it to the mails until it left on the airplane, the parcel could have been handled by as many as eighteen or twenty different people, including postal employees and aircraft loaders. As many as two dozen persons could have known that this particular packet was en route. While the million-dollar parcel was on its way across the Atlantic, the word was undoubtedly passed through criminal channels and plans were made to steal it at London's airport.

It has been learned in the course of investigation of other cases of international mail thefts that such messages are often relayed on telephone lines equipped with scramblers. These devices make conversations completely unintelligible to wiretappers or eavesdroppers, but perfectly clear to the parties at both ends. Sometimes coded cables have also been used. The so-called Australian Gang, operating from London, is known to use shortwave radio transmitters and receivers. If, as police suspect, it is they who are responsible for this mail grab, word of the high-value packet could have reached them from a pirate radio. The Australian Gang radio employs highly sophisticated cryptographic telecommunications facilities. Such equipment is expensive hardware, but it helps to protect messages from eavesdroppers. The sender types his message on a special typewriter which transfers it to a punched or magnetic tape. The tape is then placed in a coder/decoder at the sending end. The receiver has an indentical coder/decoder. These units are switched on at both ends, the message is scrambled, and then transmitted to the receiver, either by radio or telephone lines. There the message is decoded by the scrambler, transferred to tape and then printed out in clear language on an automatic typewriter.

On January 9, 1974, within thirty minutes after the flight from New York touched down at Heathrow Airport, Citibank's six-inch packet was stolen. There were several hundred parcels of various sizes carried on the same aircraft, but the theif knew what he was looking for and took little time in finding it. Within a week, the stolen checks were being negotiated at banks in Paris.

The Citibank checks were blank. Like all travellers' checks they require only two similar signatures to be acceptable at banks, stores or hotels. The passer needs only to sign the check at the top before he presents it, and then sign it at the bottom in front of the person whom he asks to cash it. If the two signatures match, he has no problems.

As soon as the first of the 1,000 stolen checks turned up in Paris, Citibank security people and French police began telephoning banks and bureaus that cash checks to warn them. In many instances they were too late; the checks had already been cashed, and often only an hour earlier. Then the gap began to close. The calls began coming in only a few minutes after the criminals cashed a check. Finally, on January 18, a clerk at the foreign exchange window of Credit Commercial de France on the Champs Elysées telephoned Citibank to report that a man was there attempting to cash two of the stolen checks at that very moment. Citibank gave instructions that the suspect be stalled and the bank doors locked so that he could not leave before the police arrived.

The man was arrested and searched. He unsuccessfully attempted to destroy slips of paper in his pockets that showed that he had negotiated five of the checks at

Société Marseillaise de Credit earlier in the day. He had only a few francs in his purse, which led authorities to the conclusion that he had passed the $5,000 to an accomplice. The $2,000 in checks he was attempting to cash was still on the clerk's desk.

This suspect glibly told the police that he was standing in the lobby of a hotel when a stranger approached him. "Look, I am from a country that has very strict currency regulations," the stranger allegedly said to the suspect. "I need someone to help me cash some travellers' checks, for which I will pay a 10 percent commission." The suspect claimed that the stranger then handed him the Citibank checks and asked him to cash them and bring back the money to the hotel, except for 10 percent which the suspect could keep.

The story was rubbish, but difficult to disprove. Without additional evidence the French police might not have been willing to hold the suspect for more than a few hours. He might have gone free had a check on his identity not been made. When the name on his passport was run through the criminal records bureau, he was found to be a known member of a gang of international thieves. Immigration stamps in his passport showed he had most recently visited Britain on January 15, and departed via Heathrow two days later.

Obviously, the million-dollar Citibank travellers' check theft was a job executed by experts working together on both sides of the Atlantic. Planning and organization were required to take advantage of a weakness in Citibank's security. Although this was the largest single haul that this criminal gang is known to have made, a detective chief inspector at Scotland Yard tells me that they pull off eighteen to twenty major jobs every year using the same method of operation, stealing between $3 and $5 million in currency, negotiable paper, travellers' checks and credit cards.

The use of bank couriers greatly reduces the risk of theft. A courier can be escorted to his flight by bank security officers and met by others on arrival. No one outside the bank organization need know that high value items are being transported. A Theft Loss Survey made by the International Air Transport Association shows that in 1,359 cases of stolen property at airports, including passenger baggage and all types of cargo, there has been no incident involving a courier. There are, however, a few cases of loss involving dishonest couriers travelling by car or rail.

Security precautions for transportation of high value goods vary widely, but in general the level is not very high. Management executives need to take the question of security more seriously before significant improvements can be made and the opportunities for international criminals reduced.

The rules of the game have been altered. What troubles many average people is no longer the moral objection to doing wrong but the fear of getting caught. Such is the case of the back office manager at a New York stock brokerage firm who programmed the computer to automatically siphon funds from a company account into two customer accounts, his own and his wife's. He milked the firm of nearly $250,000 over an eight-year period. His employer was so fascinated by the *modus operandi* that he helped his manager cover up the $250,000 loss and then became his accomplice in a new crime. Together they found a way to put their own computer in communication with the computer of a rival firm. Then they literally had their computer talk the other one into transferring the rival firm's money into a dummy bank account until they had siphoned off enough of the rival's resources to force it into bankruptcy.

Firms in Western Europe and America are being bilked out of millions of dollars every year by criminals using international mail frauds. One of the most common frauds is the sending of bills for unordered services, such as listings in trade directories and biographical blue books. According to James Robertson, a U.S. Postal Service law enforcement official, his office receives fifty to sixty complaints a day from businessmen and celebrities who have received fraudulent solicitations.

In a typical instance of this scheme, a bill for anywhere from $25 to $500 arrives in the mail from a firm in a foreign country, requesting payment for a listing in a directory, advertising book or imitation *Who's Who.* Sometimes a proof sheet showing the entry, made up from text copies of legitimate reference works, is included with the bill, but more often the tricksters do not even bother to send that. Proof sheets cost money and reduce their profits. The schemes work because careless employees of businesses receiving such solicitations often pay the fraudulent bill without checking to determine if the service was ordered.

"Sucker" lists are compiled from various legitimate sources—other directories, membership lists of organizations and even telephone books. Over 100,000 users of Telex services in the United States received fraudulent solicitations for listings in an *International Telex Subscriber's Directory.* Tens of thousands of these users automatically sent off payments of fifty dollars for their listings. The letter and the bill were cleverly designed to mislead them into believing that this was an official Telex service.

Postal services in the United States, Great Britain, France and Canada have charged more than 135 companies in other countries with alleged use of the mails to defraud with these kinds of schemes. The offenders include firms in Australia, Belgium, Great Britain, South Africa and West Germany. They run little risk of real punishment, however, as long as they do not try to bilk people in their own country.

The law and the public seem unable to move fast enough to keep up with the schemes of the new breed of electronic criminals.

The German magazine *Der Spiegel* recently reported that a man accused of fraud reaching into the millions was accommodated in a private room in a hospital instead of a jail cell after his arrest. There he was able to receive visitors and conduct his business as usual by telephone. He even made a deal to sell an airplane from his sickbed. He made a successful escape, probably with the aid of accomplices. As this is written, he is still wanted, but no one seems to be looking very hard for him.

By contrast, there was, at the same time, a man awaiting trial at Butzbach prison. He had obtained 45,000 marks as a loan in order to buy a house for his family and was accused of giving false information in order to obtain the loan. After spending months in a cell awaiting trial, he was convicted and sentenced to ten years. The harsh treatment was influenced by his prior record. Years ago, when he was fifteen, he took someone's car for an evening joyride and returned it unscratched. For this he was branded a juvenile delinquent, and condemned to wear the stigma of a common crook for the rest of his life.

Similar cases reflecting apparent injustice can be found throughout the world, and it is the elite electronic criminals who benefit from such attitudes.

In the closing years of the twentieth century, our world has been enriched by technology, but it is also in grave danger of being controlled by the modern criminal, who uses his knowledge of advanced technology as his chief tool. We become aware of his existence only on those rare occasions when he is caught. Unfortunately, such thieves meet with few failures.

2

The Art
of Illegal Entry
Made Easy

A torrential rain was buffeting London as I drove to the Hilton Hotel on Park Lane. The only parking place I could find for my car was next to the employees' entrance. To avoid getting wet I went into the hotel through that door. There was an Irish guard at a desk. He did not look up from the copy of *Private Eye* he was reading as I went in. I found my way to the lobby through back corridors intended only for the use of hotel staff. No one challenged me.

It was still raining two hours later when I finished luncheon with some business associates. I retraced my steps to the employees' door. The same guard was still on duty, bent down behind his desk tying his shoelaces. I brushed passed him. It was only as I was unlocking the door of my car that I realized the significance of what had just happened. I went back inside the hotel and walked up to the Irish guard and asked him if he knew who I was.

"Can't say I do, sir," he replied.

"Well, I'll tell you. I belong to the IRA and I have just planted a bomb on the seventh floor that will blow up in fifteen minutes. What are you going to do about it?"

He studied my face for a moment and then replied, "Nothing, sir. If you had really put a bomb there you wouldn't be telling me about it, now would you?"

Since my work takes me into many cities and towns throughout the world where security is important, I began looking for security breaches just as criminals might. They systematically look for gaps everywhere they go in order to find out how or when valuable property is unprotected. The observation that a building guard takes a coffee break at 10:15 every morning, leaving his station and hiding his heavy bunch of keys in a paper bag in an unlocked drawer, provided an art thief with the loophole he needed to get inside a Sutton Place apartment building on New York's East Side. He made off with a Corot and a Vermeer without being seen. Some months later, when he was on trial for another theft, he told the jury how easy it had been to gain access to the Sutton Place apartments.

I made it a point to visit that same building one morning at precisely 10:15. I found no one at the reception desk. The lobby was empty. I took the opportunity to pull open the drawer of the guard's desk and looked inside. There was a sack full of keys. In spite of the theft the guard's routine remained unchanged.

The following illustrations of breaches of security are excerpted from a notebook I have been keeping for several years:

● Insurance company, Newark, New Jersey: Filing cabinets locked at night but open during the day, and unattended while staff is at lunch.

● Airline ticket office, Brussels, Belgium: Combination required to open safe penciled on wall beside the safe. I tried it and it worked. Safe contained cash and hundreds of blank airline tickets. The loss to the airline for each ticket could have been as high as $1,000.

● Computer center near London, England: Unguarded side door hooked open to allow employees to step out for fresh air. Top secret military and industrial information was stored in the center's files.

• Research laboratory, Massachusetts: Seven different doors unlocked and unguarded during morning and evening hours when staff arrives and departs. At all other times the doors are locked and the area patrolled by guards.

• Computer center, Holland: "This door to be kept locked at all times" sign painted on door from which lock has been removed.

• Armored car delivery service, Massachusetts: Widely available remote-control devices used to open garage doors also open entry gates to money storage vaults. Some of these devices can be tuned to open any remote-control locks using very low radio frequency ranges.

• Management consulting firm, Switzerland: Adhesive tape applied over lock to main entry door to allow workmen to enter after hours to redecorate offices. Workmen departed at midnight but tape was still on door the following Monday morning when staff arrived. Door was open for two days over weekend.

• International airline, Paris, France: Guard at the side door of the airline's office building did not collect my visitor's pass. "We take them in at the main entrance, but it is now locked," he explained. So I walked away with it in my pocket. I used it the next time I visited the building to gain entry without otherwise identifying myself.

Identity cards are the fashion today and are accepted universally even if they are worthless. Not long ago, at London's Victoria Station, I bought myself a new I.D. card from a vendor who had set up shop in the forecourt. He took my picture with a Polaroid camera and then asked for some personal details, which a typist typed on a card as I gave them. I signed the card, which was then bonded permanently with my photograph between two sheets of acrylic. The whole process took two minutes and cost me less than three dollars. The card shows my picture and the following information:

NAME: J. Christ
ADDRESS: 1 St. Peters Gate, Heavenly Acres, U.K.
OCCUPATION: Superstar

The typist did not blink an eye as I gave her this information. I never intended to use the card for anything more than a conversation piece, but one day I accidentally presented it instead of my bank check card when cashing a check at a supermarket. The clerk merely glanced at my picture and accepted my check.

Although these do-it-yourself I.D. cards are not proof of identity, a criminal can easily link his face to a variety of aliases. The backing paper used in the cards is engraved and resembles portions of banknotes. They look so official that many shopkeepers find them more reassuring than driver's licenses or other more legitimate documents.

This I.D. card scheme is the brainchild of a former Scotland Yard Fraud Squad detective named Michael Franklin. He was aware that, whereas many countries have compulsory identity cards there are many others that do not, and a voluntary I.D. card which links personal information to the bearer's photograph is much needed for routine security checks. Obviously they are valuable to the deaf and mute, diabetics, heart patients, and others who may not be able to identify themselves in life-and-death circumstances.

An official-looking I.D. card might get you past a security checkpoint, but it certainly will not open any locked doors. For that you need another piece of equipment which can be bought in shops in most cities of the Western world. It is the Autopik, a handy device with which anyone can open 70 percent of all locks in use in the world, including those on doors, safes, automobiles and file cabinets.

Autopiks are shaped like handguns, but instead of a barrel they have detachable picks. There are two types. The first, the pick gun, opens cylinder locks having any type of pin or tumbler system. It fits all keyways and is not harmful to any part of the lock mechanism. Pulling the lever or trigger moves the pick downward and then upward with a rapid motion which effects quick opening. The second type is the rake gun, which is designed for difficult cylinder locks. When the handle is pulled the rake slides forward until peak of projection is reached. The rake then springs backward to its original position, raking the pins so that the tumbler can be turned. A tension wrench comes with each gun. It may be applied either at the top or bottom of the keyway. By applying very light pressure on the tension wrench in the direction that the lock should turn as the gun is fired, the lock turns at the moment the pick or rake forces the pins clear.

The Autopik is marketed as a "necessary addition to any locksmith's tool box," and it is supposed to be sold only to authorized locksmiths and security agencies. However, it is obviously a handy timesaver for burglars and industrial spies as well. The criminal gangs in the United States have been using Autopiks for several years. They have no difficulty buying them. I bought one myself from a mail-order house for twenty-eight dollars. The company that sold it to me had no idea who I was or how I intended to use it.

Autopiks have recently appeared in Europe. The first one turned up by police was found in a kit of burglar tools in France in 1971. Since then police have discovered half a dozen, most of which have been confiscated and put to use by police themselves. To my knowledge, more than a dozen consulting intelligence agents have them, and two of them have loaned me their Autopiks to add to my exhibit of the "tools of industrial espionage." It is a clever device and one more example of the way modern technology aids today's criminals.

One day I made a wager with the chief security officer of a well-known office machine company that I could gain access to his heavily guarded company headquarters building and get away without being stopped. We agreed that the winner would receive a bottle of champagne.

A few days later, I attempted to get by the guards by joining a hundred or so employees who were streaming through the gates into the building at the end of the lunch hour. I was stopped. Next, I tried to drive a rented delivery van through the gates into the receiving area. The guard at the gates let me in, but when I parked at the loading dock and tried to enter the building another guard stopped me. My third try was to enter the visitor's reception area without showing identification and without an appointment, but it also ended in failure. My luck changed when I noticed that each morning at about 9:30 several important company executives arrived in chauffeured limousines and were admitted without challenge by the guards. I promptly rented a limousine along with a chauffeur's hat. The next day I was in the line of limousines. When my turn came to stop in front of the entrance, I left the limousine running and hopped out carrying an attaché case. I ran into the building waving the case, calling to the guards, "He left this in the car." This time they let me go inside. Within a few minutes I found the office of the chief security man. It was empty, but I saw his red leather appointment book on top of his desk. I put it into the attaché case and hurried back to the limousine. As I brushed past the guards I waved the case again and said, "He didn't want it here today."

Later that morning I telephoned the chief security officer and told him he owed me a bottle of champagne. He refused to believe that I had entered and left the building, even when I told him I had his appointment book. He accused me of bribing someone to bring it out to me. I suggested that he meet me at the entrance at lunch time.

When he came to meet me, I asked the guards if they recalled seeing me pass that morning.

"Oh, yes sir!" one of them replied. "You're the chauffeur for one of our executives. He had left his case in the car and you brought it in for him, but he didn't want it."

The chief security officer took the guards strongly to task over the incident and I felt sure that the performance of these men would be closely monitored in the future. I returned his appointment book, and for my trouble I received a good lunch, a bottle of champagne, and a check to cover the expense of hiring the limousine and van.

It is hard to believe how easy it is to get into the room at the Bank of England where £5 million is handled daily. The designers of this facility used Fort Knox as their model. They wanted to make the currency sorting room as unpenetrable as possible, without interfering with the work. The end result is a security system that has been so modified and compromised that it offers very little protection. Still Bank of England officials point to it as their "little Fort Knox," which suggests that they are unaware of how little effective security exists.

Inside the bank is a larger busy room where clerks sort foreign currencies. At one end of the room is a vault. The vault usually contains nearly $5 million worth of foreign banknotes. In its original design, every time a clerks needed to put sorted packets of currency into the vault or take out more to be sorted and counted, the vault door had to be opened. When this was observed to be very inefficient a schedule was arranged. The time lock on the vault was programmed to be opened at three pre-set times each day. At those times, about $500,000, enough money to keep the clerks busy for two or three hours, could be withdrawn and dumped on the sorting desks.

It is clear that the existence of this schedule represented a security breach. All the clerks certainly knew at what hours the vault would be open; an outsider would have no trouble obtaining that information. In fact, when I was taken on an escorted tour of the bank's facilities, my guide told me the vault opening times. If I were a criminal and wanted to rob the Bank of England, that would be useful information. I would need only to gain access to the currency room when the vault was open, and getting into that room seems to pose no problems.

Between the main stairwell, open to almost anyone, and the counting room are two electrically bolted doors. The would-be thief could easily walk past the bank guard, who was a thoroughly bored fellow the day I visited there, and climb the stairs to the Foreign Money Sorting Department. The first electrically bolted door bars his access to an outer office, but a push button sounds a buzzer inside. Since it is assumed that no one would push that button unless he had authority to enter, the electric bolt snaps back almost at once. Once the intruder is in the outer office only one more door stands between him and the vault. There is also a push button beside this door.

Bank of England regulations require the doorkeeper inside to verify the credentials of anyone who wishes to enter before releasing the bolt. If he is satisfied, he can open the door by pushing another button on his desk. If not, he can telephone for a guard. Since the doorkeeper must open this door at least 150 times a day, and since no unauthorized person has ever tried to come in, he has developed a reflex action. When the buzzer sounds, he does not even bother to look up to see who it is. He simply reaches for the button and presses it. The door opens; the thief is inside.

I could not believe it was possible, but it was and I did it. There I was standing inside a vault containing millions of dollars with a bewildered look on my face, wondering what to do next.

"Is there something the matter?" the doorkeeper asked me.

"I . . . I was just looking for the men's room," I replied.

"Well, you won't find it in here," was the reply. I left, wondering how the bank's directors would feel if they knew how easily their vault could be entered.

Business offices are often just as vulnerable as the Bank of England. The woman in the reception room is supposed to screen all visitors and issue passes to them, but that is only one of her jobs. She must also type envelopes, answer the telephone, arrange flowers in the room, keep the magazines neatly arranged, hang up visitors' topcoats, bring them coffee or tea and take orders for sandwiches and snacks for executives who want to eat lunch at their desks. In addition, she has to sign for packages and letters, make reservations for dinners and theater tickets when V.I.P.'s are being entertained and collect money for the office football pool. She also relieves the operator at the office switchboard when called upon.

After a few people managed to get inside a particular office without being seen by the receptionist, that company installed an alarm on the main entrance door. A chime rang each time someone opened the door, but the noise of the chime so unnerved the receptionist that she switched it off during the day. So much for that security measure.

Three years ago, myself and three others were asked to help test the security at a computer center just outside Paris. The four of us—all total strangers to the firm—spent an entire day in the place, mixing with the staff of over sixty data-processing workers. No one asked any of us if we had a right to be there, although we were not wearing plastic identity badges like everybody else. I later asked a senior programmer why he had not challenged me. "Because that is not my job," he replied. "That is the work of our security policemen."

In mid-February 1974, a mentally disturbed man entered the studios of Radio Luxembourg. He carried a gun and a bomb in his pocket. The reception guard let him in, thinking he was a late arrival they were expecting for an audition. The man wandered around, talked with employees and sat at a console in an empty control room, throwing switches and turning dials. It was not until he fired his gun into the air that anyone took special notice of him. When he announced that he was prepared to die a martyr, the police were called in. He was sent to the hospital for a psychiatric examination.

Security breaches can be expensive and dangerous and almost any security system involves elements of inconvenience to employees. This is why firms must be careful in the way they institute security measures. Visible signs of security devices such as closed circuit TV cameras can harm employer–employee relations and destroy morale.

Some of the common feelings about security control among employees are:

Employee Resentment: Particularly if they feel the measures the employer has taken imply that management doesn't trust them, or if the measures seem to unnecessarily interfere with job functions, employees may experience and express resentment. After having been victimized, some firms overreact and install every available security aid. "Big Brother has just moved in and I'm moving out," said a junior executive at a Pennsylvania company, as he handed in his resignation. The firm had just spent $350,000 on a security system, which was described in a local newspaper as "tighter than a maximum security prison."

When the head of a Hollywood motion picture studio, suspecting violations of trust by members of his staff, brought in a guard service to eavesdrop on telephone calls and read the contents of wastepaper baskets picked up in the offices each night, employees retaliated by filling their wastepaper baskets with hundreds of sheets of scratch pad paper on each of which was written the words "Fuck you!"

Tolerance: If the employees realize that a company has to take measures to protect its proprietary information and property, they are more likely to accept security measures. Such workers realize that security controls also protect their jobs; the history of breaches shows that workers are often let go after heavy losses of company secrets and competitive advantages.

Curiosity: When a new electronic access control system using a coded plastic card that fits into a slot was introduced at an international airport in West Germany in 1972, employees wanted to know how it worked. The system was installed to open all entries and exits to the restricted areas of the airport that are under customs supervision. Some employees peeled their cards apart, others opened the boxes behind the slots into which the cards were placed to open gates or doors. Soon the entire system was in a shambles. Half the plastic cards were mutilated, the sensitive mechanisms were damaged, and the cards could not be read. Many employees discovered how the system could be bypassed and how easy it was to modify any card to serve as a "master key." The result was that the system had to be abandoned. It was dismantled and sold to a parking lot firm. Curiosity about the techniques and hardware used in security systems has often broken the system. This fact has led to growing interest in systems that can operate without employee awareness that they are being used.

Boredom: The monotony of standing in line to pass security checkpoints has often led to breaches. At one computer center in Illinois, staff workers became so annoyed with the bother of being screened at a guard desk every time they went in or out that they unlocked an emergency fire exit door in an unguarded conference room and used it instead. So did a saboteur who tried to start a fire in the computer tape files.

Frustration: Following an armed robbery in which two employees were shot, the management of a chemical and dye company hired a number of off-duty policemen and prison wardens as guards. They were all big, solid, rough-looking men who took their jobs very seriously. They patrolled the area as if it were a cell block and became known privately as "the boss's robots."

A company rule prohibited the use of alcoholic beverages on the premises. One day the work of the offices was completely disrupted when a "goon squad" of these guards searched everybody's desk for contraband whiskey. An extreme case, perhaps, but it illustrates that if security is impersonal, inhuman or automatic it produces feelings of frustration. In this case, a delegation of employees confronted the managing director and threatened mass resignations if the guards remained. He complied with their demands, and the guards were replaced with less oppressive, professional security men.

Generally speaking, when a security system proves to be inconvenient to the people who are guarded by it they will find ways to circumvent it; but if the system is a good one and handled correctly it can be a boon to employee and employer alike.

3

Games Swindlers
Can Bank On

In the not so recent past, fraudulent schemes were confined to confidence games, bunco, and other types of quick buck swindles, but, with the development of a technological society, this has changed. If you decide on a career as a swindler, you could easily be $2,000 richer by this time tomorrow.

Whether they are paper, plastic or metal, credit cards and bank cards* are among the most widely used products of modern technology. If their abuse became vast enough, one could say without exaggeration that the result would be the bankruptcy of our entire banking system.

THE BANK CARD CHECK FRAUD

VICTIMS:　Any bank that issues bank check cashing cards to its customers.

VILLAINS:　Anyone with a checkbook and a bank card. Although it involves greater risk, these can be genuine documents rightfully in the possession of the holder and

---

*Bank cards are documents, similar to credit cards, which are issued to bank customers to facilitate cashing checks in shops, hotels and business places, and when travelling in foreign countries. Each card identifies the customer by signature and account number, and the bank guarantees to pay any check cashed with this card up to a stated amount.

bearing his or her own name. Although there may be no possibility of criminal action, the victimized bank can sue the customer in civil court to recover the loss. Stolen or fraudulently obtained documents are used in the majority of cases. These are often sold in bars, public places and through criminal channels.

PROPS: A checkbook and bank card issued by the same bank, and transportation to a foreign country. The Euro-cheque bank card is the most widely used in Europe. Over one hundred banks in Common Market countries supply these cards to depositors, and tens of thousands of retail and service firms will honor them, since payment is guaranteed under Euro-cheque arrangements with the banks. Many credit cards—Access, Barclaycard, Bank-Americard, American Express, Carte Blanche and the like—also have check guarantee privileges.

The signature on the bank card is compared with that on the check by the firm to which it is presented. The swindler who uses a stolen bank card need not forge the signature. He can write the name in his own handwriting simply by altering the signature on the card. The signature on a bank card is written on a white painted rectangle on the plastic surface of the card. If an attempt is made to erase the signature, the paint is removed to expose the words NOT VALID—NOT VALID—NOT VALID on the plastic underneath. This precautionary measure can be easily bypassed, however, if one paints over the signature and uses the newly blank white space to write the name in his own handwriting.

The materials needed for this operation can be obtained at any office supply shop. They are liquid correction kits used by typists and are sold under trade names like Tipp-Ex, Snopake and Liquid Paper. Each kit contains two small bottles, an opaque white correction fluid and thinner. The signature area on the bank card is first blocked off with masking tape. The correction fluid is then carefully brushed over the signature, leaving a fresh, white surface. If the application of the correction fluid causes the ink of the original signature to run, the area can be easily cleaned down to the plastic card base using a small amount of the thinner.

Thousands of fraudulently obtained and stolen bank and credit cards are altered in this way every month. The technique was made possible by an advance in technology, the correction fluid, which was not developed until a few years ago.

THE PLOT: The villain must travel to a foreign country to cash the checks with the bank card since to do so in his home country makes him liable to criminal prosecution. There is a limit on the amount he can obtain with each check, set by the issuing bank and sometimes printed on the card, but there is no limit to the number of checks he can cash in a day. If the limit per check is twenty-five dollars, one morning in a large city with a book of thirty checks can net $750. One swindler equipped with three checkbooks scored $2,100 in a single day in Brussels.

This scheme may sound incredible, but it is perfectly workable. Business people and banks pay out without reservation since their money is guaranteed by the bank issuing the card. As with credit cards, lost or stolen bank cards are listed on "hot sheets" that are widely circulated to people who may be cashing checks with the cards. However, two to three weeks may elapse between the time a missing card is reported and the publication of the hot sheet. Furthermore, many employees cash checks without checking the hot sheet to see if the card in question is listed.

The fraud is not discovered until a phony check is returned to the bank. The bank must pay, but the police can take no action unless it can be proved that the crook conspired to defraud the bank before he left his home country. This charge is virtually impossible to prosecute if the swindler works alone. Often, however, the scheme is operated by a gang. In one case, over fifteen people planned their operation in Great Britain before they descended on several Continental cities. They were caught after returning home. When the conspiracy was proved in court, they were convicted and are now serving prison terms.

Because banks are reluctant to disclose the extent of their losses, no total figures on this sort of crime are available. However, I do know of one case in which an American toured the capitals of Europe working this fraud. He went home with over $600,000 and is now enjoying it, as he lives beyond the reaches of the relevant law.

This fraud is comparatively easy to carry out and bankers know it. In fact, several American, British and German banks as well as credit card organizations have retained the services of a consulting firm in Holland to meet regularly with organized crime operators and to buy back lost and stolen cards that have come into their hands. The selling prices are negotiated on a case-by-case basis by the two parties. A packet of a hundred American Express cards was sold back for $500. The same number of Euro-cheque cards fetched $350. The price on Access cards was only $50 per hundred until it became possible to use them outside of Britain. Now the price has jumped to $300. The Dutch group had reclaimed some 300,000 cards in this manner by August 1973. This is only 1 percent of the estimated 300 million bank and credit cards that are now in circulation in Europe and America. If even this small percentage were used to fraudulently obtain cash, it is clear that it could cost the issuing firms billions of dollars.

This estimate is supported by the *Nilson Report,* a privately circulated bulletin that authoritatively assesses business problems for subscribers. "The time is near," the October 1972 *Report* states, "when credit cards will become a more lethal weapon for organized crime than the gun."

The check card swindle is only one of a group, often referred to as the Euro-Fiddles, that is causing concern within the business community. It may be instructive to explore the methods of some of the other hoaxes in this group.

THE TRUCKER EURO-SWINDLE

VICTIMS: International trucking and hauling firms.

VILLAINS: Truckdrivers and filling station employees.

PROPS: Fuel credit cards or standing company accounts.

PLOT: Trucks hauling goods in foreign countries need to be refueled. To avoid the risks of giving drivers cash to pay for fuel and repair services, many international hauling firms establish accounts with chains of filling stations and garages so that the drivers can charge gas, oil and services. Haulage firms are defrauded by their drivers with the help of filling station operators, who send invoices for more gasoline than is supplied. When the fuel dealers receive their money they split the overcharge with the drivers.

An English truckdriver, Thomas V. Chessman, confessed in 1973 to three charges of giving false information for gain in a Halifax court in January 1974. Two of the charges involved conspiracy with garage operators in Koblenz, Switzerland, and the third with an operator in Malines, Belgium. His only excuse was that he was forced by the garage operators to cooperate. Chessman was fined $200.

Inquiries I have made among truckers and filling station operators support Chessman's story. If drivers refuse to become accessories to this fraud the operators may pour water into their tanks.

Mr. Ian Pollard, the prosecuting attorney in the Chessman case, stated, "This case is just the tip of the iceberg. We are now in the days of the Euro-swindle and the police have been carrying out substantial investigations into similar cases, but because they are on the Continent they have found it very hard to bring charges. They have been investigating the present case for a year and were only able to bring it to court because the defendant chose to plead guilty."

The losses sustained by this swindle by one British

transport firm amounted to about $100,000 in a single year. One driver told me, off the record, that he receives more money from the cut he gets from filling station operators than he does in his pay envelope. "This is hard work, and I wouldn't stay with it if I couldn't rip off the extra money."

Preventing the Fraud: Fuel tank meters for trucks and other vehicles have been developed. They are tamperproof and record every gallon poured into the tank. At the end of a run, the meter can be read by a company official and a record kept for comparison with the invoices from filling stations. If the total billing exceeds the amount of fuel pumped in, the trucking company can challenge the invoice.

Some large transport firms maintain their own depots throughout Europe, so that their trucks are refueled only from company-owned pumps. A few trucking companies load cans filled with sufficient fuel for a run aboard their trucks so that the driver need not buy any fuel on the way. However, this not only cuts down on the payload that can be carried, but also violates highway safety ordinances in some countries.

Perhaps a more effective protection against this type of fraud would be to issue fuel vouchers to drivers. Sufficient vouchers to cover the anticipated needs for a single run could be issued at the start of each trip. At the end of his run, the driver would have to account for any that he used and return the remainder.

STOLEN AIRLINE TICKET RACKET

VICTIM: Commercial airlines, travel agents, travellers.

VILLAINS: Organized crime.

PROPS: Stolen airline tickets. These blank flight tickets contain one to four coupons each which, properly prepared, could be used to make four separate flights between over one hundred airports throughout the world. A single coupon could be used for more than $1,000 worth of air travel. The average is about $300 per coupon. The tickets can also be quickly exchanged for cash if presented at airline offices for refund.

PLOT: Professional criminals bribe drivers of trucks who transport shipments of tickets from printing plants to airlines to turn over to them a few boxes of blank tickets. About 500 blanks may be taken from a shipment of 20,000. Such a quantity may not be missed for months. Through the channels of organized crime, these tickets are marketed at discounts to shady travel bureaus, to clubs and organizations planning group flights and tours, etc. They are also used by mob members for their personal and business travel. If the serial numbers of stolen tickets are discovered by the airlines before they have been used, they will blacklist those tickets and refuse travel to anyone who presents them. The loser in this circumstance is often the innocent traveller who bought his ticket in good faith.

The multimillion-dollar racket in stolen airline tickets started as a Euro-Fiddle, with British, French, Dutch, Italian and German airlines the first victims. In the early 1970s, it quickly spread to the United States. In the spring of 1974, Pan American World Airways paid agents of organized crime over $50,000 for the return of 2,000 ticket blanks. If used those tickets could have lost the airline up to $2 million. This unusual deal was sharply criticized by other airlines and by Franklin Oelschlager, director of the Air Transport Association, who called it "buckling to blackmail." Pan Am officials said it was "simply good business." The action is believed to have encouraged additional thefts, since airlines have created an illegal market for their own tickets.

Alfonse Confessore was a repairman from Long Island who bilked the Diners Club of over $600,000—perhaps a great deal more—by making duplicates of that company's credit cards. His job was to repair and maintain the embossing machines used to impress the names of cardholders, account numbers and expiration dates on blank Diners Club cards. The process was controlled by a punched tape that was prepared in the Columbus Circle offices of the credit card company and supplied to an embossing firm with a sufficient number of blank cards, plus a few extras to take care of rejects. It was these extra cards that made trouble. When an embossing defect was noted by an inspector, a new card was made and the defective one destroyed. Every aspect of the process was organized according to the best security practices.

Confessore had a long-standing ambition to be accepted into the Mafia family in New York. By carefully studying the stamping process for Diners Club cards, he eventually spotted a loophole in the security which would help him realize his ambition. Workers in the embossing plant had tried to steal a card or two, but they had always been caught by the strict accounting procedures. However, since the embossing machine ran automatically, no one regularly supervised it. This enabled Confessore to be alone with the machine from time to time. He made these moments pay off by throwing the lever that embossed a second card. Each time the machine produced one card for the Diners Club, Confessore pocketed a duplicate; he was not searched.

He then got in touch with some friends with Mafia connections and in due course opened a pipeline through which he marketed the cards. No one will ever know how many cards he fed into that pipeline, but, for three or four months, hundreds of top members of the crime syndicates financed their activities with those cards. They bought airline tickets, paid for hotel rooms and meals in first-class restaurants, rented Cadillacs and Lincolns, supplied themselves with fine wines and whiskies, and adorned themselves and the women in their lives with expensive jewelry. Eventually, however, the legitimate holders of the original cards complained that they were being billed for items that they had never bought. Diners Club executives, aware that duplicate cards were in circulation, hired Jack O'Toole, a former special agent of the FBI, to find out who was making duplicate cards and how they were being distributed. O'Toole had established contacts within the Mafia, and within a short time he received a tip from one of his informers: The duplicate cards were coming from the same company that made cards for Diners, a business machines corporation in Queens.

With the help of law enforcement agencies, O'Toole started investigating. After they narrowed down the list of suspects to Confessore, they had to play a long cat-and-mouse game before enough evidence was obtained to place him under arrest. A jury found him guilty on twenty counts of fraud and one of conspiracy—for which the penalty was a mere four-year prison term. Confessore never lived to go to jail. He was freed on bail to await sentencing, but, on November 24, 1969, his body was found in the street near the Jamaica, Queens, railroad station. There were three bullets in the back of his head. Had he been killed on orders from the Syndicate? No one knows. It remains one of New York's many unsolved murders.

Any major credit card company will confirm that, where Confessore left off, other criminals have picked up. Not many of them have had the opportunity to produce genuine duplicates as he did, but this has not stopped them. Plastic credit card blanks are not difficult to counterfeit, and they can easily be embossed with a portable machine that costs about $150.

A bartender in Amsterdam, Holland, and a taxi driver in Brussels, Belgium, both offered to supply me with any major credit card—American Express, Diners, Bank-Americard—issued in my own name, for about ninety dollars. They said it would take a day to make delivery. An agent for American Express once bought a gold "Executive" Amex credit card from a hotel bellboy in Miami Beach, Florida, for $150. It was a perfect fake. What was really astonishing was that American Express had not yet released their gold card. Whoever made up the fake obviously had inside information.

The bulk of the illicit credit cards in circulation are lost or stolen items. Workers in airline terminals, hotels, restaurants and other public places frequently find wallets containing one or more credit cards. They often know people who will buy the cards for resale to criminal organizations, or who use them to make purchases for themselves. A barber in Rome who found a credit card on the floor under a chair just vacated by an American tourist used the card to buy $4,000 worth of airline tickets. He took his family to the United States to visit relatives—and then sold the card to a mafioso for thirty dollars, because he did not want to get caught with it in his possession.

Lost and stolen cards have a short life. Sooner or later they appear on hot sheets. Once a card appears on a hot sheet it is not safe to use. Many professionals who trade in stolen credit cards or who regularly use them obtain copies of every new hot sheet and check their cards against the numbers on it. They keep using the cards until they are blacklisted. Hot sheets are not difficult to come by. Employees of some firms who receive them in the course of business make photocopies of each new list as it comes out and will sell them to anyone who will buy.

A blacklisted card may still have value. With the aid of an embossing machine it is sometimes possible to alter the imprinting on the card.

TRAVELLERS' CHECK FRAUD

VICTIM: Banks who issue travellers' checks.

VILLAIN: Usually a gang that makes a living at stealing and negotiating travellers' checks, but sometimes a loner who has obtained a few checks.

PLOT: Blank travellers' checks are stolen from banks and other places where they are sold, such as hotels and department stores. Stolen checks are then transported to some distant place to be cashed, either by the thieves or by accomplices working with them. Well-known criminal groups who have operated this theft and fraud include the Australian Gang, in Great Britain and Continental Europe; the Florida Gang, operating on a world-wide scale; and Black September, a Middle Eastern, politically inspired gang of extortionists, saboteurs and criminals. The fraud is not discovered until the stolen checks are returned to the issuing bank for payment, although the serial numbers of stolen checks are often known soon after the theft.

The travellers' check is a kissing cousin of the credit card. It has the advantage of being honored in more places than credit cards, and it is more easily negotiated both by the user and the businessman who accepts it as payment. The face value of the travellers' check is guaranteed by the bank that issues it. American Express, Bank of America, First National City Bank, Lloyd's, Barclay's, Deutsche Bank and Bank of Tokyo are a few of the many banks which offer the service.

Travellers' checks are as good as cash almost every-where in the world. For many years the theft of travellers' checks has been an increasingly popular crime. Professional gangs steal hundreds of thousands of dollars' worth of blank checks every year in many major cities of the world.

The history of the infamous Australian Gang is filled with incidents of travellers' check thefts. They are as good a group of fiscal criminals as ever existed. As the result of the combined efforts of Scotland Yard, Interpol, the police forces of at least four countries, and American Express Special Agents, key members of this dangerous gang have been neutralized.

In one incident, a man entered a well-known bank in London's West End. He proceeded to open his trousers and urinate on the plush wall-to-wall carpeting. While everyone watched him in shocked amazement, an accomplice reached through a cashier's window and stole a large quantity of blank travellers' checks. No one could remember seeing the theft, but over $16,000 worth of checks were missing and began to be negotiated later that day in Brussels.

A young woman stood in line at the cashier's window of an Amsterdam bank. In her hands she held a small transistor radio. Suddenly she turned up the volume, saturating the banking room with deafening rock music. She pretended to try to turn it off, but the control button came off in her hand. In the midst of the noise and confusion, an accomplice in a remote part of the bank vaulted over a counter and stole an entire tray filled with blank travellers' checks and currency. This time bank officials saw him, but they were unable to catch him before he escaped in a waiting get-away car. The young lady slipped away before police arrived. Both were later identified as members of the Australian Gang when they were apprehended in another caper.

A man entered the London branch of a well-known American bank, just before closing time. As he was crossing to one of the cashier's windows, he suddenly collapsed on the floor with what appeared to be a heart attack. While the bank's staff and customers were busy watching or ministering to this apparently very ill man, his accomplice slipped a long pair of telescopic pliers from under his coat, extended it across a counter and picked up $26,000 worth of blank travellers' checks. These checks were flown by the gang to Italy, and when the banks opened in Rome the following morning other members of the gang started to pass the stolen checks. This time, however, their luck ran out. The report of the incident in the London bank was carried on Reuter's press wire and was published in Rome newspapers while the gang was cashing checks. Employees of several banks sent Telex messages to London requesting the numbers of the stolen checks. By midafternoon, when the Rome banks reopened after lunch, half a dozen banks had a list of the check numbers. When four members of the gang attempted to cash more checks, they were stalled while police were called. A witness from the London bank was flown to Rome. He identified two of the suspects in a police line-up. One was the man who had suffered the heart attack the day before. Under questioning by police, the suspects admitted that other members of the gang were waiting in a hotel room. They, too, were arrested. One of them was the woman who played the radio in the Amsterdam bank.

Banks and financial institutions are victimized by other kinds of confidence games that produce even greater losses. Cunning, collusion and technology have replaced shotgun tactics. Banks in Britain alone are losing as much as $20 million a year to thieves. The American Banking Association estimated bank losses from fraud, embezzlement and other crimes totalling $130 million in 1972 alone.

Banks have always been favorite targets for thieves, but one wonders why some bank robbers risk their lives and a long term in prison for a piddling $2,000, when with a little more cunning and skill they could walk away with a hundred times that amount.

In 1973, there were 313 bank stickups in New York City, as compared with 182 the year before. The combined loss totals just over $2 million, and only 51 percent of these cases were solved. (The records kept are, however, selective; the losses are probably higher.)

During one bank fraud in New York City, a single thief took $1.5 million from the Union Dime Bank. In 1973, only 27 percent of the cases of embezzlement involving banks were solved.

The degree of planning that goes into bank robbery is quite remarkable, and there is evidence that banking institutions need worry less about amateurs with guns than supercrooks who live in deluxe homes and lead otherwise respectable lives. A recent wanted list for bank criminals, published by the United States Treasury Department, lists 674 persons. Of these, nearly one third were wanted on embezzlement charges, and of that group 120 were data-processing personnel: thirty-two operations vice-presidents and managers; twenty-nine loan officers; fourteen bank presidents; and so on. The total number of data-processing personnel involved in bank embezzlements during the previous seven-year period was only fifteen.

The first trial of computer-assisted bank robbery in United States Federal Court was conducted in 1966. Although the names of the villain and his victims are a matter of record, it serves no useful purpose to further publicize them.

OVERDRAFT FRAUD

VICTIM: A United States bank whose deposits are insured by the Federal Deposit Insurance Corporation.

VILLAIN: A twenty-one-year-old computer programmer.

PLOT: The villain was in temporary financial difficulties and had been turned down by the bank when he asked for a loan.

The programmer was not employed by that bank, but he happened to work for a firm that was under contract to operate the bank's computer until an in-house staff could be trained. To raise the funds, he inserted a patch* in the computer program that supervised his account. It instructed the computer to ignore overdrafts in his own checking account. Since he thought he would need the money for only seventy-two hours and intended to pay back the money and erase the telltale program patch he felt that no serious crime was involved. He wrote a check and drew out the money he needed, but his plans did not work out as he intended. Ninety days later the patch was still in the program and he was overdrawn by nearly $2,000. At that time, the bank's computer suffered a mechanical failure. Bookkeeping was transferred to a hand operation while the computer was being repaired. A clerk discovered the overdraft and alerted bank officials. The young programmer was convicted but, because of his age and the fact that he had no prior criminal record, he received a suspended sentence. This is the first recorded case in banking history in which a person not employed by a bank was convicted of altering bank records. It is an indication of the risk involved when banks bring in outsiders to handle their work.

*A temporary correction in a supposedly faulty computer program.

It is also interesting to note that, in order to appease the bank, the contractor discharged this programmer as soon as his computer fiddle became known. Once the trial was over, however, this same contractor rehired him. To do so they had to top the bids of other firms who had read about the case in the newspapers and who wanted his services as soon as he was free to go to work. Good programmers were difficult to find in those days.

PREVENTING THE FRAUD: An analysis of this case points up areas in which the bank could improve the security of its vulnerable computer. When the bank turned down the programmer for a loan its officials should have realized they had a potentially disgruntled man working with their computer. His work should have been more closely supervised or he should have been transferred to a less sensitive job. Either way, the patch on the program would probably not have remained for three months.

In general, computer personnel should be warned that their work will be monitored and the data files checked at unannounced times by outside auditors. This would make many of the people in these jobs fear detection and exposure and deter some of them from attempting crimes. It must be recognized that computer personnel are drawn from many other occupations and from many different backgrounds. Training in practical ethics and on-the-job discipline has successfully reduced the incidence of fiddles.

Computer-related crimes are by no means limited to embezzlement. In an era when the hijacking of aircraft and trucks is commonplace, it is not surprising to find cases of computer kidnap. The first instance of this was announced in *Computerworld* newspaper in the fall of 1971. Thieves raided a Bank of America branch in Los Angeles and carried off two reels of computer tape by mistake. They quickly recognized that this bonus could easily contain valuable bank records and that the bank might pay to get them back. They demanded a ransom payment, and threatened to destroy the tapes if it was not paid on their terms. Unfortunately for the thieves the bank had duplicates.

Since then there have been other cases of computer tape theft because criminals have realized the value of computer software. Few of these cases have been publicized because the victims were more eager to regain possession of their tapes or disks than to send the villains to jail. The security officer of a major German corporation told me, in confidence, that early in 1973 a former computer operator broke into the firm's computer center and took away twenty-two reels of tape containing vital customer and marketing data. Working through an intermediary, the thief informed the company that he wanted $200,000 for the return of the tapes. Since it would have cost them many times that amount to reconstruct the data on the tapes, the firm paid and got its tapes back.

Three more recent cases of software theft for ransom were reported to me, in confidence, by persons with direct knowledge of the incidents. A ransom of nearly $1 million was paid for software snatched in Japan. The ransoms paid in the other two cases—both in the United States—total nearly $320,000. No police investigations have been made in any of these cases because the victims did not file complaints. One of my sources, the vice-president of a soap and detergent manufacturing corporation, said, "We decided not to bring in the police after consultation with the company that made our computers. They suggested that if the case were to go to the courts it would get publicity which could give ideas to other dishonest people. This could produce an outbreak of similar crimes." This selfless motivation may have been quite genuine, but a banker whose firm had also paid a ransom for its software gave a more credible explanation. "Our security was lax, and we did not want the public to know how easily the thief got away with our data bank. The records of many of our good customers were in those files. If they were to learn we had been so careless in protecting this information about them there would have been hell to pay."

Not all technologically assisted bank robberies are computer-related. Another case illustrates the serious risks that are incurred when another form of technology is employed as a tool of crime.

FRAUD BY TESTED CABLE

VICTIM: One of the largest American-based international banks.

VILLAIN: Supervisor of the bank's cable remittance department in New York City, a trusted employee who played the horses and borrowed money from loan sharks to finance his betting. Deeply in debt he was under pressure from his debtors to pay up or else.

PLOT: In 1971, the loan sharks, who are linked with organized crime, put this man on the spot. One morning he received an envelope containing a newspaper clipping reporting the discovery of a corpse floating in Brooklyn's Sheepshead Bay. The story said that the man had probably been murdered because he had welched on a debt to the Mafia. That afternoon a suave young enforcer called on him. After alluding to the news story, he demanded that the bank employee settle his debt.

The man broke out in a cold sweat. He could see himself floating in the bay. At that point the enforcer suggested an alternate solution.

"All you have to do to repay your losses is to send a little cable for us to a Swiss bank, and we'll wipe out your debts."

The man agreed to the plan. He was instructed to authorize the cable transfer of $1 million from the New York bank to a numbered account in the Zurich bank. He sent the message over the bank's Telex system as a tested cable.* There was nothing extraordinary about the transac-

---

*The key to a tested cable is the code number that precedes the message. If you know how to develop the code number you can send as much money as you like to any bank in the world that uses this system—80 percent of them do—and that bank will pay the money as you direct. To prepare the code number for sending a tested cable the sender needs a code book in which certain items of information have numerical values. For example, if the transfer is from the Chemical Bank, New York City, U.S.A., the numerical values might be Chemical Bank, 6; New York City, 111; U.S.A., 27. The values are then added and the sum, 144, is sent by Telex to a bank in another country. The specially trained cable expert at the receiving end decodes the number and checks the items against the known numerical values in the code book. Numerical values are assigned for the transmitting bank, the city and country in which it is located as well as for the receiving bank. Values have also been established for the kind of currency transmitted (dollars, francs, guilders, etc.), the date of the transaction and the total amount of money that is involved in the transfer.

tion. Transfers of even larger sums are handled in this way as part of normal bank routine.

Happily for the New York bank, a newly hired woman decoded the test number—it was correct—but she did not understand the payment instructions. A Zurich bank and an account number were indicated, but the particular branch of that bank was not mentioned. She showed the Telex to one of the bank's officers who brushed it aside disdainfully. She was still confused, so on her own initiative she transmitted a Telex back to New York asking for clearer identification of the branch of the Zurich bank. The cable was received by a clerk who worked in the perpetrator's department. When he was unable to match the inquiry with any Telex message the New York bank had sent, he brought the matter to the attention of a bank officer. Thus, because of a stubborn but conscientious junior member of the Swiss bank's staff, $1 million was saved.

Many other banks have not been so lucky. Although exact figures on losses through bogus tested cables are difficult to obtain, a statistician who works with the American Banking Association estimated that it easily runs into millions of dollars every year. In 1973, a fraudulent transfer of funds was made from a bank in Paris to one in Chile. The money, over $300,000, was traced to a revolutionary political activist group who probably used it to finance their operations. The money was never recovered and the police were unable to uncover any further clues.

There is nothing new about tested cables being used against the banks that developed them. In *The Code-breakers,* reporter David Kahn cites the case of David Hermoni, an employee of the branch of Hollandshe Bank-Unie N.V. (Amsterdam) who allegedly had access to the bank's code book. It is said, he opened two small accounts in a Zurich bank and, two months later, sent tested cables to two New York banks, instructing them, on behalf of the Israeli offices of customers at the New York banks, to transfer sums totaling $229,988 to the

Zurich account. They claim Hermoni then made a quick plane trip to Zurich, presented his credentials and withdrew $200,000 from his accounts. Before he returned to the banks for another $25,000, however, a confirmation of the bogus cable was sent by one of the New York banks to the Hollandshe Bank-Unie in Haifa. Bank officials quickly identified Hermoni as the culprit and arrested him.

Another form of fraud against banks that is being increasingly used by villains is the checkbook fraud. In the following case we not only find out how this dirty work is done but also learn how police, for a change, employed modern technology to foil the plot. They bugged a bank clerk.

CHECKBOOK FRAUD

VICTIMS: A bank and one of its depositors.

VILLAIN: A criminal who works in collusion with a bank clerk on the inside.

PLOT: The bank clerk, who has access to depositors' records, locates an almost dormant account containing a large balance. The clerk then makes a photocopy of a canceled check drawn on that account and prepares new blank checks bearing the account number. These materials are then passed to the villain, usually someone who is a skilled forger. The forger makes out one of the blank checks for about two thirds of the funds on deposit in the account. The check is then presented at another branch of the bank by the forger or an accomplice carrying phony but legitimate-looking identification. On presentation of the check, the villain tells the cashier some story about needing the money at once. The clerk telephones to verify that sufficient funds are on hand to cover the check, and "blocks" that amount on the account. Then the money is handed over and the villain vanishes. After collecting, the villain usually pays the inside bank clerk 10 percent.

A London woman, Mrs. Lesley Clarke, was asked to participate in a checkbook fraud against the Kensington

Olympia branch of the National Westminster Bank, where she is employed as a bank clerk. She did take part, but with the cooperation of the police, who fitted her out with a wireless microphone/transmitter and a tape recorder.

According to the transcript of evidence presented at the Old Bailey trial on September 17, 1973, Mrs. Clarke had become friendly with a man whom she knew as Guy Darrel. He managed a rental agency in North Kensington and had found another woman to share Mrs. Clarke's apartment early in the summer of 1972. It is alleged that Darrel, who was actually a disc jockey named John Gardiner, suggested to Mrs. Clarke that since she worked at a bank she could make some extra money by taking part in a "bank fiddle." She claimed that she said that she wanted nothing to do with the plan, but that a friend of Darrel insisted that she come along to a Bedford public house and meet "the top man." With reluctance, Mrs. Clarke went.

There she said she met a salesman, Charles Da Silva, and with him two associates, a car rental driver and a demolition worker, and together they outlined to her their plans to operate the checkbook fraud, and persuaded her to help them. If the plot was successful, they said, she would receive $2,250.

What the gang did not know was that just before she went to the public house to meet them she had visited a police station, where detectives had "wired her for sound" so that they could eavesdrop on the meeting. The bugging equipment was installed in her handbag.

As the meeting was breaking up, police appeared and placed the men under arrest. Further arrests followed as the men in custody named accomplices. All were charged with conspiring to cheat and defraud the National Westminster Bank.

A related style of fraud is found in the so-called "treasury agent swindle." which first appeared in Canada about fifty years ago, then spread to the United States, where it became well known to Fraud Squad detectives in many cities. Recently it has sprung up in Europe. The method is similar, except that, instead of the check being forged and cashed, the victim is persuaded to write a genuine check and use it to draw funds from the bank account.

This fraud is based on enlisting the aid of "public-spirited citizens" to trap dishonest bank employees. Of course the one who is really trapped is the "public-spirited citizen."

Two or more villains are involved, because this fraud requires much groundwork before the victim is exploited. The team of villains moves into a town, often in a late-model luxury car. They move into rooms in a first-class hotel. Then they start doing their research.

First of all, they seek to prepare a list of potential victims. The qualities they look for are: over sixty years, live alone, with money in the bank. A sixty-to-seventy-year-old widow who has inherited her husband's estate is ideal for their purposes. Since many such women own property in middle-class neighborhoods, the villains begin their research by touring the town until they find a middle-class residential section. The street names are noted, along with addresses of the homes.

Next, they go to the local office where property records are kept and look for the names of owners of homes in these streets. Whenever they find the name of a lady listed as the owner they jot it down. Widows and spinsters are often the only ones who hold property in their own names. With this list in hand, the villains consult the local directory or town hall records to find out the ages of the ladies. Any one under fifty-five years is crossed off. At this point they have perhaps three or four "semifinalists."

Now a very important part of the fraud begins— picking the victim. One of the villains is usually a specialist at what is called "qualifying." He also speaks several (European) languages. Posing as a treasury agent or a bank inspector, he telephones the potential victim, the first step in setting up. The villain follows a script similar to the following, which was obtained as evidence against one man who was apprehended:

"Hello, Mrs. Good? This is your bank calling. We are having a little trouble in the accounts. I hope that you can help us. Do you have your bankbook handy? Would you get it please? I would like the date of the last transaction in your book. Fine, that checks with our record. Now what is the last balance in your book? Thirty-nine thousand, five hundred and forty. That's fine. Your account is correct."

If the amount is too small to interest the villains, the lady is told, "Thank you. Sorry to have bothered you, good-bye." But, if she has enough in her bank account to make it worthwhile, the villain's voice drops almost to a whisper and he begins talking to her very confidentially:

"Mrs. Good, are you alone? Are you free to talk? My name is Holmes, Madam, S. Holmes. I am a state banking inspector. We have been called to investigate some irregularities at your bank. We suspect that one of the cashiers is an embezzler. Would you cooperate with us in trapping this dishonest person? It may interest you to know that the state offers a substantial reward to persons, like yourself, who assist us in these matters."

If she agrees, she is told to go to her bank at a certain time the next afternoon—usually on a Friday, for a reason that will become apparent later. She is to withdraw a stated sum of cash, a very large amount, and take it home in a sealed envelope. If she complains that because of her age she does not get around well, the villain offers to send a taxi to take her to the bank and return her to her home.

In any event, he states that a bonded messenger will call at her home and collect the envelope of money so that it can be checked for fingerprints and serial numbers by the bank examiner. He also tells her that the money will be returned to her account and a deposit slip mailed to her home.

This all sounds quite legitimate, which is just the way it is intended to sound. And if the lady leads a life that doesn't have much excitement she may jump at the chance to play "cops and robbers" like they do on TV. When a victim really seems to get into the spirit of the thing, the villain may suggest that she wear gloves, to protect the fingerprints on the envelope she receives from the cashier.

On the day of the payoff, the victim is kept under continuous surveillance by the team of villains. One watches her home, one is stationed outside the bank, a third may be inside the bank, while the fourth is standing by in the nice-looking car ready to play his role as the "bonded messenger."

The reason for this surveillance is that there is always the risk that the victim will become suspicious and inform the police or bank officials. The villains in the team are in continuous communication with each other by walkie-talkies, a useful technological aid.

If the victim is seen to make a false move, such as receiving visitors at her home who look like police before or after her trip to the bank, or if she engages in a long conversation with any bank employees when she goes to cash her check and take the money, the watching villain can give a signal to his accomplices and they will promptly abandon the game.

However, if all goes well for the villains, she will bring the money home. The messenger will arrive soon after to pick up the money and give her a receipt. He will reassure her that as soon as the bank examiner has checked the envelope and banknotes the money will be put back into her account. If she has been promised a reward, that money will be added, and the bank will send her a deposit slip.

Payoff day is usually on a Friday, or the last day before a long public holiday period, since the banks will be closed for two or more days. The victim will not be able to inquire at the bank until the next week. By then the villains will have moved on to another part of the country and already be making preparations to set up another elderly victim.

In 1972 a team of villains made a swing through France from Nice to Paris, operating this fraud more than thirty times. Their total haul was nearly $420,000. Behind them they left a trail of old ladies whose financial security had been wiped out. Three members of this gang were killed in a motorway crash on a foggy morning in West Germany. Evidence of their crimes was found by police in papers in the trunk of their automobile, along with banks where they had deposited their ill-gotten gains. Only half of the cash remained, but that was returned to the victims.

What surprised the police is that a number of the women who had been swindled never reported their loss to local authorities or to their banks. Some of them said they were too embarrassed at having been "taken in" to tell anyone.

PREVENTING THE FRAUD: Senior citizens and others who are vulnerable to being victimized by con men could benefit from the experiences of those who have suffered such losses. They can learn what to do if they find themselves being "set up." One bank in California that has many old people as its customers has reprinted news items and magazine articles on frauds against the elderly in a little booklet which it sends to depositors. As a result, some twenty-eight villains who attempted to victimize these people were arrested with the cooperation of local police.

Banks do have, at the very least, a moral responsibility to protect the interests of elderly customers with substantial accounts. Some banks "flag" these accounts, so that any unusual activity is brought to the immediate attention of a responsible officer.

BAHAMAS GOLD SWINDLE

One of the newest frauds has become very successful because of the strong public interest in gold, stimulated by publicity about the gold market.

Victim is observed by villain as he stops to look at one of the displays of gold coins in windows and counters of banks, money exchange bureaus and shops for coin collectors throughout Europe. If the intended victim appears to be a prosperous business executive or a tourist with plenty of money, the villain approaches and starts to admire the coin display with him. They usually get to talking about gold and the villain says he knows where some gold bars can be bought cheaply for resale at the going market price. He invites the victim to come with him while he sells two gold bars that he has just received from this source. If the victim is seriously interested, he goes with the villain to a legitimate buyer of gold.

There, the villain sells 2.5-pound standard gold bars, which are absolutely genuine. When they leave the shop, the villain tells the victim how much profit he made on the sale—by which time the victim is already showing interest in a gold deal for himself. The villain invites him to go to a coffee shop and discuss it.

From his pocket, the villain produces a brochure which he has paid a printer to run off for him. It explains how to buy gold from an organization in the Cayman Islands at far below the market price. To qualify, the buyer must be able to purchase a lot of gold bars that costs $20,000 and must be introduced by someone who has done business with the firm.

The villain agrees to provide the introduction, and he persuades the victim to take advantage of the opportunity without delay, pointing out a line printed in the brochure: "Offer subject to cancelation without notice at any time."

If the victim hesitates, the villain offers to send a cable to the Cayman Islands to find out if the offer still stands. The reply, which comes from an accomplice of the villain, states that the offer is being withdrawn in forty-eight hours. Any orders received with cash before the deadline will be honored.

"Listen, let's go over to your bank now and send your order right now," the villain says. "I've done this before, so I'll go with you to help you cut the red tape."

If the victim bites, his money is being transferred to a bank in the Cayman Islands within hours, addressed to the villain's accomplice with instructions as to where the gold bars are to be delivered.

Then the victim sits back and waits for his gold to arrive. He waits and waits and waits. By the time he becomes suspicious the villain and his accomplice are long gone.

The gold bars used by the villain as props for this fraud were bought by him at full market price. He loses something when he sells them, but his loss is more than covered by his profits from the fraud.

One American businessman who fell victim to this fraud on Via Veneto in Rome informed a U.S. consular officer that he had been taken for $300,000, and the records at his bank support his story. Even a banker was victimized—for $40,000!

The Cayman Islands are only one of several places in the Bahamas used as contact points with accomplices in gold swindles.

Of course, the banks in these cases are only unwitting tools of the con men. But, without their high-speed money transfer services, villains would not be able to separate victims from their money before they realize what is happening.

Anyone familiar with the way banking is actually done can detect loopholes which can be advantageous to cunning villains. Some of these provide ways to obtain more money than by gold swindles, and with much less trouble.

FORGED SHARES FRAUD

If all the villain needs is some security for a loan from a bank, forged stock certificates are as good as real ones and cost very little. Any job printer can run off excellent fakes for almost any company listed on the stock exchanges. Thanks to recent advances in graphic arts technology watermarks, embossed stamps and other devices placed on share certificates to defeat forgers are readily duplicated. Engraving plates and intaglio finishes can also be duplicated.

The villain can turn these into money very quickly. A

warning that fake stock certificates were flooding money markets followed the discovery in 1972 that more than 100,000 shares of one of Hong Kong's largest firms, Hutchinson International, with a market value of $HK 1.8 million, were forgeries. Trading was suspended in this stock until a search for more fake certificates could be completed. Meanwhile, other fakes were discovered in Hong Kong. Investigations revealed that lax conditions governing registration of shares made it possible to infiltrate forgeries when brokers and registrars were snowed under. Tighter regulations govern transactions on Wall Street and at other major stock exchanges, but these rules do not cover banks who "hold" a borrower's stock as collateral.

Many banks grant large loans without checking to find out if the shares put up by the borrower as collateral are genuine. If the loan is paid back, the shares are returned and no one is the wiser. It is only if you have no intention of paying back the loan that you should take a long vacation abroad.

These are serious—and wide-ranging—matters. One bank executive in Brussels told me: "For all I know there is a forged share certificate for every genuine one in our vault." It did not seem to worry him.

4

Stolen Shares
and
Bank Accounts

The theft of stocks and bonds is a thriving business that has largely been taken over by the crime syndicates. Anyone who has visited the back rooms of stockbrokers, or the back offices in banks will remember seeing stacks of valuable certificates open on desks. Sometimes they are not moved for a week or ten days while clerks catch up with their paperwork. Messengers walk about financial district streets carrying fortunes in old battered briefcases. The opportunities for robbery are many, but most of the thefts are "inside jobs."

Jerry Wolf was a Wall Street financial house clerk who owed $5,000 to a loan shark, Nathan Sachen. The debt was payable at $250 weekly, including a 5 percent weekly interest. Jerry was having trouble raising the money and claimed he had been badly beaten on one occasion for welching on a payment. He alleged that after being threatened again and being forced to supply three other customers for the loan shark, he went to the New York District Attorney's office. From that time on, all of Jerry's meetings with Nathan Sachen were electronically recorded. Ultimately the surveillance paid off.

Here are extracts from the New York City District

Attorney's transcript of those conversations. They tell their own story:

SACHEN: You have stocks in your possession?

WOLF: Yes.

SACHEN: And I want you to sell the stocks.

WOLF: Right.

SACHEN: Can you handle that?

WOLF: Sure.

SACHEN: Can you handle it without being found out?

WOLF: Sure. We receive stock certificates every day. Sometimes they are not correctly made out, and I have to send them back to transfer agents for correction. I can show that shares were sent back and take them and sell them.

SACHEN: Do they investigate this? Do they find out if the certificates were really sent back to the transfer agents or not?

WOLF: Not until maybe six months later.

SACHEN: What happens then?

WOLF: The auditors find that it is missing and query the transfer agents and the clearinghouse, and they find out who bought the stocks. An investigation gets started.

SACHEN: And eventually it comes back to you. What do you say when you are asked about it?

WOLF: I say that the names were incorrect on the certificates and that I sent them back to the transfer agent. My books back me up. The stock certificates disappeared, were lost, strayed or stolen after they left me. I'm not in any trouble. Whoever is the owner of record on the stocks—whoever bought them and has them—will carry the burden of suspicion.

SACHEN: Let's say I want to sell some stocks. Is there any legal way to do it?

WOLF: I have the rules and regulations of the transfer agent at home. I'll read it.

SACHEN: Good. Now here is what you can do for me. There is a possibility that you can wipe this debt out to everybody's satisfaction, that you can come out of this clean, owing nothing. You understand?

WOLF: Yes.

SACHEN: I know a guy who can maybe handle the stocks. But, you understand, it has got to be done very discreetly. If anything goes wrong you're the one that is going to be hurt. You're the one that it will all fall down on. You'd be dead, D-E-A-D, dead!

WOLF: I understand this.

SACHEN: You'd better never forget it. As far as anybody else is concerned, *you* stole the stocks, *you* made the sale. Nobody else. As far as I am concerned I never saw you before in my life. You understand?

WOLF: Yes.

Some time later, Detective Henry Cronin, an undercover expert in the New York District Attorney's office, contacted Nathan Sachen. He posed as a buyer of stolen securities and opened negotiations. Their conversations took place over the telephone, which was tapped by police. The following transcript starts after the conversation had been in progress for several minutes:

CRONIN: . . . I know that as of now that stuff is still hot shit. But we will take it. That is my man will take it. And what about what you said before that you had some other hot stuff, too. You see we're going to have to sit on this other for a long time.

SACHEN: Let me tell you what is available beside this, which is what you're trying to get. I mean, you want to make the big score.

CRONIN: You bet your life.

SACHEN: All right. There is a quarter to half a mil available beyond this.

CRONIN: You don't say?

SACHEN: Yes.

CRONIN: Well, that's good. Because we do a good business without taking any chances. We don't want the underworld in on this. What we do with the stock is legitimate business.

SACHEN: Well, you understand it's from them. It's from them.

CRONIN: It's from the underworld?

SACHEN: Right.

CRONIN: . . . Remember when we discussed the deal at first you said you had two or three big ones.

SACHEN: Part of it is gone.

CRONIN: What about the over-the-counter stuff?

SACHEN: I don't know if that is still available.

CRONIN: You said that we could have that, too.

SACHEN: Right.

CRONIN: At the same price?

SACHEN: As of closing today. Make it today—then there's no problem.

Detective Cronin made an appointment to meet Nathan Sachen on the following Tuesday in a parked car on a busy street for the final exchange of the stolen securities. The police had also bugged the car with electronic gear.

SACHEN: Now the man that's going to be coming is my partner. . . . He is not a gunman. He's a boss in the upper echelons. You understand?

CRONIN: Un-huh.

SACHEN: This is a man like me.

CRONIN: He is a man you can trust? He knows about the deal?

SACHEN: My associate. He's been my associate all of my life. He's never been arrested in his life. I've never been arrested in my life.

CRONIN: Does he know what's going on?

SACHEN: Absolutely, he's part of the deal.

CRONIN: That's what worried me about Jerry Wolf. He's been away.

SACHEN: He's been away?

CRONIN: No, no—I don't mean in jail. I mean he's been away from this deal. He doesn't know what it's about.

SACHEN: And he shouldn't. Because he becomes a witness with details. You see, if anything ever happens to you or your people and they get caught—let's say they make a mistake and they get caught, I assume that we have an understanding. If anything happens to us we aren't going to say anything about you, naturally. And, if anything happens to you, you are never going to say a word about us.

CRONIN: Right.

SACHEN: Whoever gets bagged gets bagged on his own, if he does something.

CRONIN: Right.

SACHEN: Now we've done this all of our lives and we've never been caught. Because we deal discreetly and we're 100 percent our word. Now if you get caught, you're going to look at Jerry Wolf. Right?

CRONIN: Uh-huh.

SACHEN: Now Jerry ain't going to say a word because he knows what would happen to him. So it will end there, you follow me?

CRONIN: Sure.

SACHEN: That's why I want you to give him a couple of extra bucks. He's your ally. Now, you want me to call the man?

CRONIN: All right. We can do it right here if you want to.

Nathan Sachen called "the man," his partner, who, police claim, brought an attaché case full of stolen securities to the parked car, and for almost an hour, Detective Cronin and Sachen's partner went over the list of stocks, comparing the items with the actual certificates. Hundreds of people walked by not realizing that a fortune was changing hands only a few feet away. But, nearby, detectives from the New York City District Attorney's office listened to every word transmitted by the "bugs" in the car. When they felt that they had all the evidence they needed, they moved in.

Here are the final moments recorded on the transcript:

CRONIN: Pacific Tel and Telegraph . . .

MR. X: A hundred . . .

CRONIN: All right, that checks it off. And you figure the total at what?

MR. X: Eighteen hundred and thirty shares.

CRONIN: Eighteen thirty. Right. That's ninety-eight thousand, nine hundred and sixty-seven dollars.

MR. X: Is that what is in this envelope?

CRONIN: Actually there is ninety-nine thousand there. You owe me thirty-three dollars.

MR. X: Here, take this fifty and we'll call it square?

CRONIN: No, I'll give you seventeen dollars.

MR. X: If you insist, okay.

DETECTIVE: Get out of the car.

MR. X: Hey! What is this?

DETECTIVE: Get out!

MR. X: Hey! Who are you? I was just talking to this man in his car. Who are you? A police officer?

DETECTIVE: Get out!

The outcome of this grand larceny was the arrest and trial of Nathan Sachen and his partners. Testimony given at the trial states that Nathan Sachen, the proprietor of a legitimate retail business, had been inveigled into marketing securities stolen from banks and brokerages because he, too, had been the victim of a loan shark.

A policeman who acts as an undercover man must use his capabilities to the utmost in order to match wits with sophisticated criminals. The purpose of undercover work is to gain knowledge of the criminal and to gather evidence against him, and to locate the source of the crime and all those who may benefit from its proceeds.

An undercover agent was also responsible for breaking the case of the deposit slip fraud, which plagued banks in New York City, Washington, D.C., Los Angeles, Boston, London, Zurich, Paris and other cities.

DEPOSIT SLIP FRAUD

VICTIM: Banks and savings and loan associations.

VILLAIN: Anyone with a knowledge of the process of printing, in language a computer can read, on deposit slips—and a desire to make money dishonestly.

PLOT: The villain opens a bank account with a small deposit. He receives the code number that identifies his account to the bank's computer on the checks that are given to him. This is technically known as the MICR-code. He then goes to the customers' desk in the bank and carries away a supply of blank deposit slips. These he prints, or has printed, with the MICR-code for his own account. Returning to the bank, he puts these deposit slips back into the racks on the counters. Then he goes home and waits for his account to fill up with money.

This ingenious fraud is believed to have been invented

in 1972 by a magazine writer who suggested it in a fiction story that was published in a well-known women's monthly. In early 1973, depositors at banks in several Eastern U.S. cities began to complain that their monthly statements were in error. Deposits which they claimed to have made were not credited to their accounts. These were honest people and the bankers knew they were telling the truth.

A consulting detective bureau was retained by a Boston bank to investigate the mystery. It was soon discovered that all the missing deposits had one factor in common: They were all made in person at the bank. None of them came through the mails.

The detective bureau sent an undercover agent to the bank. His job was to watch people do their banking. He stood in line at cashiers' windows and attempted to observe amounts of deposits and withdrawals. These he jotted down in a notebook. At the end of the day, he compared his notes with a print-out record from the bank's computer showing all deposits made that day. He found several discrepancies.

"But I saw those people put their money in the bank. Why doesn't it show on the computer record?"

Using the bank's closed circuit television system, he began to study the movements of customers. He saw them go to the counter, fill out a deposit slip, and then carry it to a cashier with their checks and cash to be credited to their account. There was nothing extraordinary in this. The trouble had to be after the deposit was turned over to a cashier. Were cashiers stealing the money?

To test this, the undercover agent opened his own account in the bank. Then he went through the steps of making deposits. Each day for a week he put ten dollars into his account. Every time the amount was duly credited and showed on the computer print-out. Then the following Monday he repeated the same process, but this time the deposit disappeared. It was not credited to his account, and not entered in the computer record. What had happened to it?

At this point word reached the Boston bank that other banks around the country were having similar problems. The undercover agent visited these banks to compare notes with security officers. They were no closer to solving the mystery than he seemed to be. On his way back to Boston he had a brainstorm.

The next day, he went back to the bank and made a deposit of eight cents. It was added to his balance. He kept on putting in eight cents every few hours, each time filling out a deposit slip and taking it to a cashier. Each time it was handled in the normal way, although the cashiers were puzzled by his actions. "I was using my own money," he said, "so I wanted to make it go as far as I could. I did not know how long I would have to wait for some action."

On the seventy-seventh deposit he again got action. His eight cents failed to appear on his account. So he obtained a full copy of the computer print-out for the day and went over it item by item. Eventually he found an account to which eight cents had been credited. It belonged to a student at a nearby university.

The agent obtained the name, address and other data about the student from the university's registrar. He was a student in the Computer Science department, an advanced program of theoretical study. The university's yearbook editor also supplied the agent with a photograph of the student. With the help of other agents from his bureau, the undercover agent placed the student under twenty-four-hour surveillance. On the second morning of surveillance they observed the student as he went to the bank. He inquired after the balance in his account, and then withdrew $1,150, leaving $50. On his way out, he stopped at a counter and stuffed a supply of blank deposit slips into his pocket. He then went to the university. After lunch, however, he returned to the bank and went to the counter where he pretended to write out deposit slips until the room was almost empty and he thought no one was watching him. Then he took a stack of deposit slips from his pocket and slipped them into the racks.

As soon as he left, the undercover agent retrieved some of those deposit slips from the rack. They were carefully examined and it was found that each one had been imprinted with the MICR-code number of the student's account.

It was now crystal clear. Any depositor using one of these slips would lose his money. The computer read the student's number on the deposit slip and automatically credited the amount to his account. Every few days the student visited the bank and withdrew other people's money from his account, and added some fresh deposit slips to the racks.

He imprinted the deposit slips on equipment to which he had access at the university's computer center.

At the time of his arrest he admitted to having obtained over $67,000 by fraud. Except for a few hundred which he had spent, the balance of the money was in a suitcase in his room. Because he made restitution, the charges against him were dropped.

A report of this case was circulated through banking channels and proved helpful in solving similar cases in other cities. But this method of fraud is so easy and tempting that it is continuing to plague banks and their customers in many countries.

DR. NOE AND THE BANK TAKEOVER

Banks change hands in the same ways that business firms do, and this can include a fraudulent takeover manipulation. Such schemes are often foiled by banking laws, and Fraud Squad investigators. The villains sometimes show such a genius for creative banking that if they only followed the rules they might well have become important bankers. There is no way to tell how many banks are taken over by illegal means; the figures would vary from country to country. Furthermore, when such takeovers are successful we never hear about it. Only when the villains get caught does the public know.

Stolen Shares and Bank Accounts

VICTIM: Privately owned banks, merchant banks, savings and loan associations, investment banks.

VILLAIN: A man with a knowledge of high finance and a criminal streak.

PLOT: Villain seeks bank that is looking for more capital to expand its operations, or one where the sole owner desires to retire from the business. Such banks often advertise their needs in "Business Opportunity" columns of leading newspapers. Once he has established contact with a suitable victim, he uses worthless securities to buy his way into the bank. Once inside, he siphons off the liquid assets and uses the bank's respectable name as a front for further frauds.

In 1964 Dr. Clifford Noe and his brother Paul bought a bank in their home state of Texas and milked it dry in a short time. They were prosecuted under federal law and Dr. Noe spent two years in prison for his sins. But evidently the first prison term wasn't long enough, because six years after he was released he went to prison again—this time in Great Britain—after failing to pull off what could have been one of the biggest bank frauds in world history.

According to the records of his trial at Old Bailey in 1972, Dr. Noe and his brother Paul organized a gang of at least twenty professional villains and established a base in London. There he found a small bank with a capital of about $700,000 that was seeking additional funds to permit its expansion. Dr. Noe arranged to meet the owner of this merchant bank, E. H. Marley and Partners. He told Major Marley that he was the leader of a wealthy religious sect in the Southern United States and that he had at his disposal their treasury of nearly $100 million. He claimed that he was authorized to invest some of this money in a sound business venture that would eventually finance the expansion of the evangelical activity of the church in Europe. It was a good story.

Major Marley had no reason to doubt Dr. Noe at the

time, for the Texan had handed over to him for safe keeping some $5 million worth of Swiss bank deposit certificates. Of course they were fakes.

Soon Dr. Noe was the banker's partner in practice, if not in fact. There still was a technical hurdle to be passed: Dr. Noe needed Bank of England authority to gain partial control of E. H. Marley and Partners. In the meantime, Dr. Noe and his brother, working with their confederates, laid plans to flood Europe with worthless stock backed by the Marley bank's good name and reputation. In addition, Major Marley signed a document granting Paul Noe authority to solicit funds in the bank's behalf and to authorize loans by the bank, providing that commissions were paid in advance. This was a very dangerous document to give to a villain. Using it, Paul Noe did in fact raise a "few odd million" with the help of his confederates in foreign countries. Then the whole grandiose scheme was foiled by a "tremendous trifle"— like the loose nail in the shoe of a horse that causes him to lose the race.

Dr. Noe enjoyed high living, but, since he had not yet established credit in London, he opened accounts at top-class restaurants, hotels and shops in the bank's name and began running up bills. When his account passed the credit limit of £300 at Omar Khayyam restaurant in the city, the management pressed him for payment. When Dr. Noe failed to send a check, the restaurant got in touch with the bank, which refused to accept responsibility for the account. The bank had never authorized Dr. Noe to open an account in their name, and the police were called in to investigate.

At about the same time, Major Marley began to have second thoughts about the document he had given to Paul Noe. He decided that he had been premature in granting such broad authority before the Noe brothers actually became his partners. He also realized belatedly that Paul Noe could be using the document to raise money dishonestly. He, too, went to the police and told them the whole story, including his concern about the document. He asked them to help him to find out about the background of the Noe brothers. Were they what they had represented themselves to be?

Major Marley's complaint and the restaurant complaint met on the city Fraud Squad blotter. Detectives began making inquiries and soon realized that they were on to something big. In quick succession pieces of evidence fitted together revealing the classic plot for a fraudulent bank takeover.

In October 1972, Judge Edward Clarke sentenced Dr. Noe to seven years' imprisonment. After considering his prior record, there is cause to wonder if he will not spend his time in jail hatching plans for a new bank takeover.

Hatching plans is apparently what Michael M. Rush did while serving four years for fraud in a prison at Toronto in Canada. As soon as he was released (on April Fool's Day 1973), he left the country. He surfaced a short time later as the general manager of an organization called National Trust Company of Belgium. It was a kind of investment bank, it seems, although it was not possible to obtain information about it from standard financial sources in Europe, Canada or the United States.

One might say, in this case, that instead of taking over an existing bank, the villain created one for himself.

The National Trust Company of Belgium had a mailing address and a telephone number, and not much else, in Antwerp. During the summer of 1973, thousands of invitations to invest in a company called Diversified Mining Corporation were sent out with a letter on National Trust of Belgium stationery signed by a C. P. Whitehead, who was identified as a director.

In the same envelope was a document described as a "confidential computer print-out" which painted a glowing picture of Diversified Mining Corporation and a subsidiary of which it owned 80 percent, Bryant and May. The print-out claimed that Bryant and May owned a number of lucrative North Sea oil and gas assets. As a result the print-out said that the value of Diversified

Mining's shares had risen to about twenty-five dollars each.

The Whitehead letter said that National Trust of Belgium was acting on behalf of an estate that needed to be quickly settled to sell 290,999 shares of Diversified Mining at a fifth of their market value, $5 a share.

When business news editors read some of the invitations, they published articles urging their readers to exercise caution in Diversified Mining. These warnings appeared in *The Sunday Times* and *The Financial Times* in Great Britain, and in business newspapers in other European countries where the invitations to invest appeared.

Further investigations, reported by Lorana Sullivan (*The Sunday Times*, December 30, 1973), revealed that these warnings were entirely justified. There is a Bryant and May, Sullivan wrote, a subsidiary of British Match, which has no link with Diversified Mining. There is also a real Diversified Mining Corporation in Canada, whose president and *sole* shareholder is one Louis Sheriff. Sullivan concludes that, if anyone did buy Diversified Mining shares—it seems likely that some people did, but no one knows how many—"they would have to be counterfeits since the only shares issued by the real company are owned by its real president."

My point in mentioning this case is to stress the techniques used by the villain. He offered the fake shares in a real company, thereby making the offer plausible. Estates do liquidate securities assets at a loss, from time to time, in order to meet settlement deadlines. That is normal. He backed this up by dropping the names of two legitimate businesses in other countries, Diversified Mining Corporation and Bryant and May. Prospective buyers of his fake stock might choose to look up these firms and assume that they are the ones connected with the offer.

But the real genius in the offer was the use of the "confidential computer print-out." It was printed on genuine print-out paper in the type style found on these machines. The paper even bore the faint imprint of the manufacturer, an internationally known computer company. This lent a priceless tone of credibility to the rubbish that was the text of the printout.

The general public, unfortunately, is still inclined to accept as gospel truth anything generated by a computer. The fact is that computers can and do tell lies whenever false data is fed into them. They are only machines that process information that is supplied by the human brain—the source of both truth and lies.

FRAUD IN FAILURES OF GERMAN BANKS?

The international financial world was shocked by the failures of several supposedly thoroughly responsible and solid West German banks who were forced to turn in their banking licenses following foreign exchange deals in which they ran up heavy losses.

The first to go under, in late June, was Bankhaus Herstatt of Cologne, one of the country's largest private banks. Other private banks, some of whom came into liquidity problems as the result of the Herstatt failure, soon collapsed as well. As worried clients crowded outside one German bank after another eager to learn if their money would be paid back, public prosecutors began investigations of fraud and violations of national bankruptcy and share regulations.

For some months before these banks were forced to go out of business it was general knowledge that they were engaging in excessive currency speculations. They were trying to make profits from the fluctuations in floating national currencies. They bought U.S. dollars, for example, when they were at 2.5520 deutsche marks and sold them at DM2.5650. Unfortunately, some of the currencies dropped in value—lower and lower—after the banks bought them and when they were forced to sell them they suffered a loss. One bank, according to a report from the government central banking union, lost DM.0150 on every dollar's worth of foreign currencies it had bought for investment. This does not seem like a lot, but the loss was repeated every day for nearly three months—$15,000 per day on each million dollars' worth of foreign currencies. This bank had nearly $12 million invested in foreign currencies. Its losses in the end totaled over $16 million, meaning that much more money than the original investment had to be poured in to cover the losses. The currencies in which they speculated were U.S. dollars, French francs, Swiss francs and Italian lire, among others.

The money which the banks used belonged to their customers, who had come to expect conservative management of their funds which in the past had made their money grow. What a shock it must have been to clients to discover that Herstatt, for example, was DM400 million in debt. Among those clients was Morgan Guaranty Trust Company of New York, which may have lost as much as $13 million in the Bankhaus Herstatt collapse. The two banks had entered into an agreement to exchange deutsche marks for U.S. dollars. On the day before the collapse, Morgan paid over DM33,183,000 to the Cologne bank out of its Frankfurt office. Herstatt, however, failed to pay over the $13 million to complete the exchange: It was already insolvent. Herstatt officials should not have accepted the marks from Morgan since they already knew that they could not pay for them. But they did, and so the question of fraud arises.

This transaction is typical of the many that the defunct West German private banks engaged in as they tried desperately to survive. The failure of these banks has had repercussions in stock exchanges, the foreign exchange market and in political circles, where the talk was of stricter regulations by government agencies.

But the impact was felt just as strongly in the home of a seventy-six-year-old German widow, Frau Lenora Faulwetter. She had entrusted DM78,000 to one of the private banks—her entire fortune. "Why did they do it?" she cried to a television interviewer. "What right did they have to play around with my money? Those bankers are no better than thieves!"

5

Criminals
on Tape

The fraudulent use of tapes is opening up a whole new world to plagiarists, thieves and manipulators. On tape recordings, words can be rearranged and new words can be built up from an assortment of syllables. The process is somewhat like fitting together bits of a jigsaw puzzle. Simply by inserting or deleting "nots" in a taped voice recording, affirmatives can be changed to negatives and negatives to affirmatives. Words can be borrowed from one part of a tape and fitted into another so the entire meaning is changed. By the same techniques, inflections of words can be altered.

Recently I listened to a tape in which the late French comedian Fernandel and Gertrude Lawrence played a scene from Noel Coward's *Private Lives.* Not only had these two performers never appeared together, but Gertrude Lawrence did not speak French professionally. But she did on this tape. The recording was manufactured by a clever Parisian sound technician from recordings of sound tracks of old films in which each of these stars had appeared.

Similar "doctored tapes" have been created for amusement and as academic exercises by tape editors in many countries. One such tape, made by Douglas Shearer, former head of the recording department at Metro-Goldwyn-Mayer movie studios in Hollywood, brought together Eddie Cantor and Barbra Streisand. Again, these entertainers of different generations had never met. In building words from syllables spoken by them, Shearer also took the opportunity to ham up Shakespeare. The voices are not smooth, and the tones are rocky, but this is what they are heard to say:

CANTOR: But, soft! What light through yonder window breaks?

STREISAND: It is the bathroom, and who left the light on?

On another tape, an ABC news editor assembled bits and pieces of the Queen of England's Christmas messages and U.S. Senator Sam Ervin's remarks during the Watergate hearings to produce this impossible conversation:

SENATOR ERVIN: Good morning, madam. I didn't recognize you.

HER MAJESTY: But I am the Queen!

SENATOR ERVIN: You don't look at all like you do on the stamps.

It is possible to do almost anything with tapes to fool the human ear. During World War II, the Germans took wire recordings (predecessor of magnetic tapes) of President Roosevelt's fireside chats. They added words here, deleted words there, and the result were F.D.R.'s "pro-German" speeches broadcast to America's allies in Britain, France and other countries. They were a powerful and effective Nazi propaganda tool.

The German trickery was amateurish. Since then, the technology of altering tapes has progressed so far that today any tape editor with a little effort can take a recording of Henry Kissinger and have him say almost anything. The technique of reworking a tape to alter completely the substance and meaning of the original words is so widely used that no one can be certain that any tape is genuine without corroborating evidence.

Courts of law in many countries were inclined to permit tape recordings to be introduced as evidence in civil and in some criminal cases, but now they are beginning to question the authenticity of tapes. Experts on tape recordings are beginning to appear and give testimony at trials, as specialists in the analysis of questioned documents, handwriting and fingerprints have been doing in the past.

One such expert is John Dean (no relation to the Watergate case figure). He showed me in less than thirty minutes how he could use his recording equipment to completely change the meaning of a conversation. The actual exchange went like this:

MR. X: Listen, Sam, you know from your talks with Tony, Lou and Harry that they knew about it.

MR. A: I suppose they did, yes.

When Mr. Dean finished editing the tape it came out like this:

MR. X: Listen, Sam, you know from Tony that he knew about your talks with Lou and Harry.

MR. A: I can't recall ever discussing the matter.

"Only a highly skilled and experienced sound engineer could detect the doctoring I just did," Dean said. "In fact, there is no sure way of telling whether a tape recording has been tampered with, unless it is a bad job of alteration. Then even a layman can spot the doctoring, as easily as a badly counterfeited banknote."

Taking words out is easier than putting words in. For this you only need an inexpensive tape editing kit sold in shops, containing a marking pencil, sharp blade, splicing tape and a jig to hold the tape while you are working on it. First, you play the tape to locate the word you want to delete. You mark the spot with the pencil and transfer the tape from the machine to the jig. Using the blade you snip out the unwanted word. Then you splice the tape together. Since the splice is evidence of tampering, the tape can be "dubbed" (re-recorded) onto a fresh reel which is uncut. This, then, can be represented as being the "original."

The difficulty in re-recording is to make the splice inaudible on playback. An oblique cut through the tape when making the splice helps. But if you are not careful, it will show up as an unnatural sound—an abrupt change in the strength or tone of the speaker's voice or an interruption in background noise.

A tape submitted at a trial in Mississippi, reported in *Tulane Law Review,* included some editing which was not apparent until a member of the jury raised a question. The recording had been made in a room where a radio was playing *Clair de Lune.* The juror, who was a piano teacher, asked the judge why several bars of the music were suddenly skipped. The tape was replayed, and the gap in the background music was verified. The judge ruled that the tape was inadmissible as evidence.

When an expert re-records an edited tape he often masks the splice sound by adding background sound effects appropriate to the situation. If the tape is supposed to have been made in an office, the masking can be done by adding the ringing of a telephone, rustling of papers, coughing, or the squeaking of a chair. If the tape has been recorded in an automobile, splices could be effectively masked by auto horns, screeching brakes, slamming car doors or other familiar—and therefore unsuspicious—noises.

It is quite easy to take out words, but it is more difficult to insert new material into an original tape. If you are an audio expert, you can construct a fake speech out of old tape recordings, as John Dean did in the above demonstration. He snipped out individual words spoken by the speaker and spliced them together into brand new sentences. Where there is need for a word that has not been recorded by the speaker, it can be created by assembling syllables. It takes time, technical know-how and the right equipment. But with those things you can make up anything.

Another method used in preparing tapes for a blackmail attempt was to hire an actor who could impersonate the voice of the person whose story the blackmailer wanted to falsify. In this case, the actor recorded on a dictating machine several letters which the victim had never given to his secretary. The impersonation was so perfect that when the victim heard the tapes he wondered for a time if he had not suffered a lapse of memory and had indeed dictated the incriminating letters. The fact that the dictating machine had poor quality recording and reproduction only made the fake more difficult to detect.

To make a genuine-sounding insert, you need the original speaker, sitting in the same room, in the same chair, with the same background noises, speaking into the same microphone and being recorded with the same tape machine as in the original.

Even when you apparently duplicate all the conditions that existed when the original recording was made, "tremendous trifles" can trip you up. For example, the speaker may be in a different mood than before. He may have been calm and relaxed when the original was made, but now he is tense and excited because he knows that a fake is to be produced. His voice may well reflect the changes.

In making physical tests to determine the validity of a tape, the investigator often uses highly sophisticated instruments. An oscilloscope can detect the all-but-inaudible clicks a tape recorder makes when it starts and stops recording. It can detect even the sound of a splice going by.

Sound spectrographs, which are machines that turn sound waves into pictures (sometimes known as "voice prints"), are also used. Many experts, and some courts, feel voice prints equal fingerprints as a reliable means of making identification. The technique was employed several years ago when Howard Hughes gave a telephone interview to reporters to repudiate the Clifford Irving biography. The question in many minds was: Did the real Howard Hughes speak? A tape of his remarks during the interview was compared with a recording known to have been made by the genuine Hughes, and these were compared by the sound spectrograph method.

In the voice prints, Hughes's spoken words were reproduced as a contour map, with the louder portions being represented darker and higher and the lower pitches as lighter and lower contours. Words spoken on both the questioned tape and the genuine recording were compared as voice prints. They were almost identical. The slight differences could be accounted for by changes in Hughes's voice as he aged. The experts certified that both tapes were made by the same person.

More recently, computers have been programmed to analyze voice patterns from recorded tapes. Such analyses can reveal characteristic and absolute magnitude of all facets of the spoken words. They can also reveal periodic signals produced by fluctuations in the human voice that are inaudible to the ear and elude detection using other conventional analytic methods, such as breathing patterns of the speaker, acoustical defects in the mouth and throat, and other "trace characteristics."

Procedures used in establishing the authenticity of a tape recording, or determining that it is a fake, fall into three categories: subjective, objective, and physical.

The *subjective* tests are accomplished by lending an ear to the questioned tape. The expert listens for audible breaks, which could indicate bad splices, erasure and re-recording or other tampering. He studies the logical content and the continuity of thought of what is being said. Does it make sense?

In addition, the investigator listens for speech flow evenness, variations in voice levels and tone inflections, and particularly background sounds. Are they consistent with the location where the recording is said to have been made? Abrupt changes in background noise arouse suspicion.

The second type of test to which questioned tapes are subjected is objective and concentrates on "fingerprints" left on the tape by the recording machine on which it was made. Machine vibration during recording can produce distortion, wow and flutter. If the "recording level" was set too low, too much noise (hiss) will be heard on playback. If set too high, distortion will be heard.

The tape noise level and identification of all signals on the tape other than the recorded material is a useful source of clues. For example, in one case the loud buzz on a tape was blamed on a table lamp and electric typewriter near the recorder. Experts were unable to duplicate the buzz with these items, but they did determine that it was caused by a sixty-cycles-per-second hum from the recording machine's electric cord that was picked up on the tape. Magnetized recording heads, tube microphonics and other irregularities also leave telltale marks on the tape.

The third and final phase of tests are physical or mechanical, a qualitative analysis of the tape itself. The investigator usually begins with a visual inspection of the tape to assess its general condition—new, slightly used or cracking and peeling from long service. He also looks for splices and signs that the tape has been tampered with. He may subject it to microscopic study for identification of abrasions left on the tape surface by recording heads, tape guides and scratches from reels. Just as every bullet is indelibly marked with unique scratches caused by the gun from which it was fired, so every tape machine leaves its marks on the tapes recorded with it.

Next the investigator compares the tape with samples of tapes from all companies who supply them, to identify the manufacturer, type of tape, date of manufacture and other facts. This can supply important clues. In a recent case the tape introduced in evidence was represented as being the recording of a conversation on October 7, 1969. On inspection of the tape, the expert determined that it had not been manufactured until the spring of 1971 and could not have been purchased before the following fall.

During a recent visit to a music shop in Nice, France, I bought a recording of *Glenn Miller Hits* (*Elmer's Tune, Moonlight Cocktail,* etc.). When I played the record at home it sounded exactly like the original Glenn Miller orchestra, although no mention of this fact was made on either the album jacket or the record labels. I had bought an illegal copy of an old favorite Miller recording. Millions of such copies of recordings are being sold every year throughout Western and Eastern Europe. Detecting these frauds with a computer, programmed to analyze sound patterns, is now the full-time business of several agencies employed by legitimate record producers—RCA Victor, Columbia, Deutsche Grammophon, Polydor, and others.

PLAGIARIZED MUSIC FRAUD

VICTIM: A famous record company that markets albums by celebrated performers throughout the Western world.

VILLAIN: A shoestring record company in Holland that markets bargain price albums.

PLOT: The villains copied recordings and packaged them in their own albums without license or payment of royalties. The labels and album sleeves gave no names of the performers, or credits to the orchestras or composers, but did feature colorful, often sexy, pictures and provocative titles to attract buyers. For example, a photo of a bosomy redhead spread out on a stack of hay was topped by the title: "Hayride Love-In—20 Tunes To Make Hay By."

With no artist's fees, recording costs, composer's royalties and expenses to recover from profits, the shoestring record company made a fortune selling the recordings at two thirds less than the American proprieter's list prices. Instead of making a criminal complaint, the American company elected to sue for damages. They estimated their losses at more than $3 million.

In a preliminary deposition before the trial, the Holland firm denied that it had copied music from the American firm's records. They admitted, however, to studying carefully the hit performances on the American recordings and to using these performances as "inspiration" in the production of their own records. They claimed the performances were by their own orchestras and artists, who were not identified because they were known performers working on the cheap.

Officials of the American firm were convinced that the Holland company had copied their records. They hired audio investigators to make a computer analysis comparing three musical selections—their own against the alleged copies. The analytical data, presented numerically in the computer print-outs, showed identical number patterns for both the genuine recordings and the illicit copies. The American firm won its case.

Plagiarism of recorded music is widespread today. Dozens of firms are successfully selling illegal copies. Many of these are in the Eastern European countries. Some of them record music played by disk jockeys on British, Luxembourg and German radio stations and stamp out records from it. These records are then sold without copyright license or payment of royalties. To defeat this practice, some radio stations instruct their disc jockeys to start the record playing while they are still talking and to begin talking again before the record ends. In order to make an illegal recording without the disk jockey's voice, the introduction and close of the music must be cut off, which reduces the market value of the records.

TYPEWRITER TAPES AID BLACKMAILERS

In 1972 the following small ad appeared in newspapers in New York City: "WANTED FOR CASH—USED CARBON TYPEWRITER RIBBONS AND ONE TIME CARBON SHEETS. Call XXX-XXXX for details." The response armed a professional blackmailer with enough inside information to make a fortune. Secretaries and typists in doctors', lawyers' and other offices where sensitive information is handled saw the ad and the opportunity to earn a few extra dollars by selling the carbon ribbons they discarded in the office waste baskets. They were obviously valueless, and their employers did not even need to be told.

But not to the blackmailer who bought them at 10 cents a ribbon. He managed to read the ribbons and one-time carbon sheets quite easily and thus learned the contents of recent letters, memoranda and other documents written by people who had private information that he could turn into big money. He even gained access to the secrets of New York City police detectives and undercover operations of the investigators of the U.S. Treasury Department's regional headquarters, when clerks in those offices sold him their carbon ribbons. A computer operator in a bank's data-processing center inquired if he would be interested in the carbon paper sheets used to make copies of computer print-outs. He was most interested, and thus obtained daily reports on the bank accounts of thousands of businesses and private persons who had accounts at the bank.

An investment of a few hundred dollars for the carbon ribbons made it possible for this villain to blackmail over twenty people and extract from them an estimated $350,000 before he was apprehended.

DICTATING MACHINE TAPES

Careless handling of unerased dictating tapes has also made fortunes for more than one villain. Service men who repair dictating machines and telephone answering machines that use magnetic tapes have easy access to inside information. Some dishonest ones have turned this into high profits.

I recently asked the repairman who came to take my broken-down dictating machine to his shop for overhauling if it was really true that his customers leave tapes on their machine when he takes them away.

Criminals on Tape

"Listening to tapes is fun," he said. He told me of some amazing things he had heard which would cause national scandals—lawyer's notes for important cases, private letters dictated by celebrities to their illicit lovers, management strategies to fight a union during an industrial dispute, executive plots to fix prices in an important commodity industry, confidential notes taped by a psychiatrist regarding his patients.

Another service man told me, in Paris, that he had listened to a tape left on a machine by a customer, who was a leading Women's Liberation advocate. "You should have heard the letter she dictated for her husband," he said. "She's a complete fraud. The other night I heard her say on television that she was liberated, and that she would never get married."

A third inquiry led to my hearing a tape on which a top official of a multinational corporation dictated a number of routine letters. Then, at the end of the dictation he added: " . . . and if you can finish typing these by five thirty, Sharon, how about coming into my office for a fast fuck?"

One office machines repairman played a tape on which an executive of a large corporation involved in bargaining with a labor union discussed the limits of money and benefits the company was prepared to offer. He copied this tape and sold the copy to the labor union for $2,500. The union, which was ready to accept lower terms, quickly revised its demands and got the maximum. During the talks, the union officials admitted how they had obtained their information.

I am amazed how apparently security-minded corporations often have overlooked such risks. At one French firm I saw a cart piled high with tapes standing in a corridor outside their mail room. A hand-lettered sign read: "Leave tapes to be erased here." The firm had a bulk tape eraser machine in its mail room and accumulated tapes during each week, then had a clerk erase them all on Friday afternoons. I could have stuffed some of these tapes in my jacket and walked off with a pocket full of company secrets.

Premature revelation of information concerning a company's annual report, that showed it was suffering heavy losses due to bad management judgment, caused rumors that raised havoc in investment circles. The leak was traced to an unerased tape of a draft of the report that had been left on a dictating machine sent out for repairs and had been sold to a newspaper reporter.

An enterprising industrial spy in Lyon, France, once put on a pair of overalls and pushed a trashcan through the offices of a large corporation. The lid of the can was held down with padlocks, and there was a slot in the top. Glued to the can was a sign: "Put all used dictation tapes, carbon ribbons and extra copies of company confidential documents in here." In a short time, obliging office workers filled up his can, clearing their desks and drawers of excess company secrets. The spy wheeled the can past guards—saying he had orders to take the contents to be burned—to his station wagon in the parking lot. He loaded the can into his auto and drove home. Then he began the laborious task of sorting out his haul. He found nothing useful for his immediate needs. But there was a tape on which someone had dictated a memo outlining company plans to cheat employees out of certain fringe benefits. The spy played the tape several weeks later at a party in his home, for amusement. One of the guests who heard it passed the information about the plans to an employee. He immediately put it on the "grapevine" and stirred up a hornet's nest. There was a general walkout of employees the next week.

When investigators traced the trouble back to the stolen tape it was found to be several years old. It had been dictated by an executive when he was employed by another company and brought along with him when he changed jobs. It had been put away in his secretary's desk drawer and forgotten until the man with the trashcan came around.

6

The
Wiretap Crooks

Thousands of tape recorders are being used by criminals every day in telephone tapping and bugging operations. They provide a permanent surveillance record and free crooks as well as legitimate investigators for other work instead of having to sit for long hours wearing headphones to eavesdrop on other people.

Tape recorders vary in size from "minicorders" no bigger than a matchbox to the massive professional units which can only be carried inside a truck or used in a "studio." Regardless of size they all have the same problem: limitation of tape time. A C120 compact cassette can only give one hour of recording time without being flipped over because ultrathin magnetic tape is used. The longest run possible, using the slowest recording speed on standard recording machines (2.4 centimeters per second—which gives rather poor fidelity), a 10½-inch professional spool of tape, and a good recorder, is only one day. This means that if you are tapping a telephone around the clock you must replace the tape at frequent intervals. Longer recording time is possible by attaching to the recorder a control device which causes it to record only when the telephone is actually being used or when a signal is being received from a bug. As soon as the transmission ends the tape stops. In this way time is saved. But, depending on how many and how long the conversations recorded last, fresh tapes must be put on the machine frequently. This need has led to the capture of undercover agents.

THE CASE OF THE GROWLING DOG

On a hot August weekend in 1972 a keen amateur radio operator in Holland picked up illegal broadcasts by an Alsatian dog named "Fritz."

Jan B., age forty-eight, spends many evenings a week talking with other "ham" radio stations across the world from the broadcasting rig in an upstairs bedroom of his home near Breda. On the weekend in question he was scanning the wavebands for someone to talk with and happened to tune into a strange signal on 93 megacycles.

It was a humming sound, an unmodulated carrier wave, showing that a radio transmitter was turned on. Jan B. knew it shouldn't be there. He thought it might be a trial transmission by engineers working on a new local station that was being set up in nearby Belgium. It interested him, so he turned up the volume and left his receiver on the channel, expecting sooner or later to hear some kind of a signal. Meanwhile, he answered some letters from other amateur operators.

"It was very quiet in the room," he recalls, "and after a time I realized that something was being broadcast over the station. I adjusted my tuner and increased the volume still higher. In the distance I could hear, faintly, the sounds of traffic—cars changing gears, stopping, starting up again."

Then, about an hour later, Jan B. heard a man's voice say: "Here, Fritz! Come here, boy!" A dog barked happily. "Time for us to get to bed, Fritz!" said the man, speaking in the Nederlands language. Fritz continued to bark from time to time in the bedroom as he and his master prepared to settle down for the night. The last thing Jan B. heard was: "Get off the bed, Fritz!" and the click of a bed light switch, followed soon by loud snoring, perhaps the man, possibly the dog.

Jan B. listened in again the following morning and heard an alarm clock ring, then the man and dog beginning a new day. An hour later, the man left the house, and the dog started to whine and growl.

Intrigued by the unusual broadcast, and with nothing better to do, Jan B. decided to play detective for the day. He tuned a small portable radio receiver on the signal and rode off with it on his motorbike. By turning the receiver and holding it at various angles, he was able to fix the direction from which the broadcast signal was coming. He put on earphones to hear better.

The trail led him south nearly twenty miles and across the border into Belgium; all the time the broadcast of the howling dog was getting stronger. He reached a point— an intersection at a small Belgian village—where he could see the automobiles that he was hearing over his radio stopping for a traffic light.

There were only a few people on the village streets at the time. Most of them were coming from the church. Jan B. stopped some of them and asked the question: "Do you know anyone with a dog called Fritz?"

"Yes," someone told him eventually. He pointed out a nearby garage. "The owner of the garage has a dog named Fritz. It's a big Alsatian."

Jan B. had a clear notion of what was going on. He made a shrewd guess to explain the unusual broadcast, and, when he found the garage owner, he said to him: "I think your home is being bugged."

"I'm not surprised," the man replied. "I'm being blackmailed."

He asked Jan B. to go with him to his house in the hope that together they could find the "bug." Taking care not to say anything that would tell an eavesdropper they were making a search—thus warning him and giving him time to escape—they went over the rooms inch by inch. Taped to the bed frame, underneath, they found the first bug. It was no bigger than a packet of cigarettes—a black plastic box that contained a microphone and transmitter. It had a long, thin antenna and wires running to a skirting board behind the bed and into the back of a wall socket, from which it was drawing its power. This was the radio that was broadcasting the signal which Jan B. had been hearing.

The garage owner wanted to rip out the bug, but Jan B. shook his head. It was better to leave it until they tried to find the eavesdroppers.

A second bug—battery operated—was found attached to the back of the telephone stand in the salon of the house. It was a "dead bug," since the batteries had been drained. The two men went to the police.

Jan B. suggested that it was likely the eavesdroppers would be found within a few hundred yards of the garage owner's home, since the type of transmitter found in the bug normally has a range of no more than a mile or two.

"There had to be some rare atmospheric conditions at the time to enable me to pick up the signal so far away," Jan B. says.

Police concentrated their search on parked cars within the village. In a green DAF Mini, about 150 yards from the garage owner's house, they found the radio turned on and tuned to 93 megacycles. A wire connected the radio to a tape recorder on the floor of the car. They played back a section of the tape and heard the growling Alsatian.

Jan B. noted that the tape reel was due to be changed in about three hours. It was a Braun machine with professional 10½-inch reels for the longest playing time. The police staked out the car and waited for the eavesdropper to bring fresh tapes.

Within two hours, a second car carrying two men stopped beside the DAF Mini. One of them, carrying a box of tape, let himself into the car and started to change the tape. The police moved in and arrested both men.

The garage owner identified the man who waited in the car as the one who had been blackmailing him. The other man turned out to be a private detective hired to set up the surveillance over the garage owner. Afterward Jan B. pointed out that, if they had not come back to change the tapes, they would never have been caught.

Tape recorders have a broader application than is generally suspected. In the same sense that computer systems employ terminals and other peripheral equipment to do their jobs, tape recorders can be fitted with a wide variety of bugging and telephone tapping instruments for undercover work. The chart on page 92 shows some typical tape recorder applications.

In the novel George Orwell wrote about the year 1984 he said: "You had to live—did live, from habit that became instinct in the assumption that every sound you made was overheard, and except in darkness, every movement scrutinized."

If he had written his book today—only ten years away from 1984—rather than in the 1940s his details would surely be more terrifying. Today there are infrared cameras that can indeed see you in the dark, even portable TV cameras that can record pictures by moonlight, and radio-controlled miniature aircraft (some that can hover like helicopters) to carry these cameras to subjects that someone wants to photograph. Today, also, everybody's private conversations can be listened to.

We need a better understanding of the threat in order to take preventive action. If telephone tapping and bugging is something we have to learn to live with, then all of us must plainly learn what they are all about and what action to take—or not to take—when a suspected tap or bug is encountered, especially when they are the tools of villains.

Let us take a closer look at the peripheral devices which can be used with tape recorders.

TAPPING A TELEPHONE

Telephone tapping is a simple matter. No special technical skills are needed. Anyone with average intelligence and the ability to use a screwdriver can learn in ten minutes how to tap a telephone. There are three basic methods: inductive pick-up devices (not directly connected to the telephone); direct-wire taps (installed in the telephone itself or between telephone and main ex-

APPLICATION	Recorder with Amplifier	FM Radio Receiver to Recorder	Portable Pocket Recorder	Sound Actuated Start-Stop Unit to Increase Tape Time	PERIPHERAL DEVICE	REMARKS
Telephone Wiretap (wired to phone). Direct-on-line *Range*: Limited by length of connecting wires	X			X	Pick-up coil or wired directly to telephone line or distribution board.	Can be detected by physical search—difficult task.
Telephone Wiretap. Wireless *Range*: 100 yards to 3 miles, depending on transmitter capability		X		X	Miniaturized microphone/radio transmitter, either a "drop in" fitted to telephone or box at any point along the line.	Quick and easy to install. No battery required. Radio signal aids detection.
Room Bug—Wired *Range*: Limited by length of connecting wires	X			X	Microphone connected by wires to recorder. May be concealed in walls, furnishings.	Takes time and expertise to install. May give better quality recording.
Room Bug—Wireless *Range*: 100 yards to 1 mile, depending on transmitter capability		X		X	Microphone/radio transmitter. May be concealed in waste basket, lamp—or disguised as electric outlet, ashtray, table lighter.	If battery is used may have limited service life. Quick to put in place given the opportunity.
Combined Telephone Tap and Room Bug (which can be monitored at long distances). *Range*: Limited only by length of telephone services used	X			X	Infinity transmitter. Fitted to telephone. May be dialed from another phone anywhere in world to pick up conversations both in room and on telephone.	Simple to install. Unless switched on, cannot be detected except by physical search.
Roving Bug—Wired	X	X			Wristwatch mike, tie-clip mike, pen mike carried on person and wired to pocket recorder.	Highly sensitive and reliable. Good quality recording. Difficult to detect.
Roving Bug—Wireless *Range*: See Room Bug above		X		X	Same as items above but with built-in radio transmitter.	More flexibility. Need not be carried.

change); and wireless radio taps (which can be picked up by any VHF [FM] radio receivers). Signals from all of these devices can be fed into a tape recorder.

The most simple form of the inductive telephone pick-up is attached to the side of a handset by means of a rubber suction cup. Other models can be placed under the telephone instrument, as a pad on which it rests, or be held in the hand of the user while making the call. The signal, passed through an amplifier into a tape recorder, headphones or speaker, produces a high-quality reproduction of the conversation. A more sophisticated telephone monitoring apparatus packages together the inductive pick-up and a radio transmitter. It is placed near the telephone and operates on its own batteries about eighty working hours with Mallory 1.4-volt batteries. This apparatus broadcasts to any normal VHF (FM) radio up to half a mile away. It operates on the international 2-m Amateur Band or between 85 and 100 M.c.p.s. The frequency is adjustable. Hazards of discovery are greatly diminished because these devices draw no current from the telephone lines and are difficult to detect by electronic means (except for the radio transmitter).

Since the telephone is a wired microphone and transmitter already, there is a wide variety of ways in which it can be tapped. The most simple direct-wire tap makes use of spare wires already in most of today's telephones. If you look inside a telephone you will see that the microphone (transmitter) and earphone (receiver) are wired through the handset cord to a terminal strip inside the body of the instrument. Often only two of four or six wires are actually used. There are often spare wires in the cable which can be connected to these terminals and used to relay conversations to some distant point— anywhere before the lines reach the main exchange— where they are connected to an amplifier and tape recorder or loudspeaker used for listening. The same results can be obtained by clipping wires to the proper terminals at a distribution board. Of course, this involves identification of the line you want to tap, which may be labeled by some obliging telephone installer. If not, you have to check every line until the right one is found—no mean task in a building which may have several hundred telephones and as many unused lines.

Another kind of direct wire tap is a radio transmitter which is fitted anywhere between the handset and the main exchange. It starts transmitting the telephone call by radio as soon as the receiver is lifted. It draws power from the telephone lines, so it has a long service life. The frequencies on which it broadcasts on the VHF (FM) band can be adjusted between 85 and 100 M.c.p.s. by turning a trimming screw on the unit.

One of the most common FM radio taps—manufacturers tell me that three million have been made and sold since 1970—is the "drop-in." It is installed in a few seconds by replacing the microphone capsule in a handset with the wireless monitoring apparatus which cannot be distinguished from the standard capsule except that a tiny screw head may be visible through one of the holes on the top. This screw is used to adjust the frequency. It operates every time the handset is lifted, drawing current from the telephone itself. No battery is required and the monitor will continue to function for a long time. One of these units has been in continuous service for seven years. I know, because it has been installed since 1967 in my own home telephone for demonstration purposes.

Recently, Dan Piliero, Managing Director of Chevron Oil Company in Holland, invited me to his office at the Hague. He asked me to bring along some of the bugs and wiretaps I had collected. He particularly wanted me to demonstrate a drop-in device.

I set up an FM radio receiver and then went to his desk telephone to drop in one of the FM radio capsules. When I unscrewed the microphone cap of his telephone handset I was astonished. "You don't need my drop-in to demonstrate wiretapping, Dan," I told him. "You've already got a drop-in bug right here."

Telephone drop-in FM radio telephone taps can be bought in New York for about $35, in Paris for about 100 francs, and in almost every city of the world at comparable prices. The radio shop in the duty-free section at Amsterdam's Schiphol Airport also sells them. To anyone who can turn a profit from eavesdropping the cost is low. It is difficult to see how the manufacture and sale of these devices could be controlled, especially since there are ethical uses for such equipment. Tiny FM radio broadcasting stations, very similar to the drop-ins, are concealed in the costumes of actors and singers to pick up and amplify their voices in large auditoriums and outdoor theaters. Paging systems for employees in a business, doctors in hospitals, officials in the United Nations, and so on make use of similar equipment.

"I cannot be responsible for the integrity of the user. . . . I don't ask him what he does with these devices," said J. E. W. Fien, division manager of the Tax Free Radio Shop at Schiphol's Shopping Centre when he showed me his case full of bugs.

"If we're serving the public, we're antisurveillance specialists; but if we're lawfully serving the law we're surveillance specialists," said Roger Boswarva, sales manager of Argen Information Services, which offers— among other services—custom-made electronic ears, eyes and memories.

Boswarva tells me that permanent wiretaps are installed on telephones in hotel rooms that are likely to be used by important people and top executives of corporations and governments. These taps are often of the drop-in variety, function as standard telephone microphones and do not arouse suspicion. Once installed, the agent often does not bother to go back and recover the drop-in. There is always a good chance that he may be interested in listening in on the conversations of a VIP who may occupy the same room at a later date.

According to Boswarva, security personnel of a business machines firm "invaded" the Paris Hilton hotel a week before a rival firm was to use the hotel for a top-secret sales conference. They had obtained a list of the rooms to be occupied by officials of the rival firm, and arranged to occupy the same rooms. Their sole purpose was to install drop-in devices in the telephones in these rooms. A week later, when the conference was in full swing, these same security people were sitting in parked cars outside of the Hilton hotel listening in to the telephone conversations and picking up valuable business secrets. One agent took a portable FM radio up to the second level of the Eiffel Tower, two blocks away from the Hilton, where he got excellent reception from one of the wireless taps that he was monitoring.

An American surveillance agency which has its taps and bugs permanently installed in key hotel suites in New York, Washington, Miami Beach, Chicago and other major cities, I am told, earned $40,000 in 1972 from selling information it picked up to newspapers and newsmagazines as "tips."

Wiretapping and bugging are standard techniques used in journalism. "It takes a bug to catch a bugger," said a member of *The New York Times* Washington bureau. News editors are eager to "scoop" the opposition, but they must have reliable information. What better information can they have than the telephone conversations of the principals involved in a story? During a visit to the National Press Club in Washington, I was told by responsible members of the press corps that many of the leaks of information about the Watergate bugging case came from wiretaps and bugs planted for the use of newsmen.

As I travel doing research, I have made it a practice to check the telephones in hotel rooms that I occupy to see if they are tapped. I have found drop-in instruments in six European hotels since 1972 in my rooms. I assume they were left in place following some previous surveillance, as I cannot think of a good reason why anybody would want to tap my hotel telephone. The hotels are: the Westbury (London), George V (Paris), Hotel Amsterdam Hilton (Amsterdam), the MacDonald (Brussels), Intercontinental Hotel (Düsseldorf), and Holiday Inn (Zaventem Airport, Belgium).

Several leading multinational corporations recently circulated memoranda to their executives "blacklisting" numerous hotels throughout the world following checks by their security personnel. In many instances a hotel made the blacklist because the check revealed "permanent" wiretaps on some room telephones. Executives of these firms, the memoranda stated, are forbidden to use these hotels on company business without permission of the internal security chief.

In August 1974, a professional surveillance agent employed by a news bureau in Paris managed to obtain an invitation to a party aboard the yacht of a Greek industrialist. The yacht was moored in the port of Monte Carlo in the shadow of the palace of Prince Rainier and Princess Grace. This agent took on board in the pockets of his tuxedo several tiny FM-radio bugs and taps. During the course of the evening he installed them at various points and in the cabins of the yacht, including the radio-telephone room. The Greek owner of the yacht was actively concerned with politics in Greece and in the explosive Cyprus situation. By monitoring the telephone and radio communications from the yacht, the news bureau was able to learn of important behind-the-scenes developments days ahead of its competition and to accurately predict the actions of key figures in the Greek government.

INFINITY TRANSMITTER

While the drop-in tap is cheap enough to be expendable, there are more sophisticated devices that sell for $1,000 and up. For example, there is a terrifying family of devices known as "infinity transmitters." This is a device which you hook up to your own telephone. Then you can dial any number, regardless of distance. An electronic tone oscillator deactivates the ringer of the distant telephone and opens up the microphone. This allows you to hear any sound within earshot of that telephone without the instrument being taken off the hook. But it only works on numbers that you can dial directly, not through switchboards. I once hooked up an infinity transmitter to a telephone in London and dialed a number in Los Angeles, the office of a former business associate who has a direct line to this desk, I heard his voice as he gave dictation to a secretary as loud and clear as if he were in the next room.

What is ironic is that people are only slowly realizing that such sophisticated telephone tapping is possible. I have had intelligent people argue with me that infinity transmitters are impossible, that they cannot be made to work. What they forget is that the standard telephone is such a simple instrument, with only two wires connecting all of its functions to the trunk lines in most cases, that protection against effective wiretapping cannot be built into conventional telephone instruments.

Furthermore, the infinity transmitter bypasses the toll counting devices in telephone offices, so that the user is never charged for the calls he makes with the equipment. Telephone companies around the world are being defrauded of millions every year by users of infinity transmitters.

An executive I know in Brussels bought a pair of infinity transmitters for about $2,000 and sent one to his boss in California. Now they can talk for hours over international telephone circuits without spending a penny for the service. Before they started to use the equipment, their telephone bill ran at least $2,000 a week.

"With the cost of telephone services going up every few months, the infinity transmitter purchase has proved to be a sound investment," this executive told me. "It helps keep down our overhead."

Nearly 25,000 infinity transmitters are in use around the world today, based on figures obtained from the six principal suppliers. Of course, there are many more, as I have no reports on the numbers of custom devices that have been made or on the sales of the transmitters produced in Eastern Europe and Japan.

Many infinity transmitters have been bought for use with computer systems in order to avoid the telephone line charges between terminals at distant points and computer centers. One manufacturer of computer hardware has built in an infinity transmitter in the peripheral units it produces which "talk to computers" over telephone lines. This fact was discovered by telephone company investigators who were trying to find out why the billings to customers who are computer users were lower than would be suspected. Although these were obvious cases of fraud against the telephone companies, they were settled amicably in most cases. The infinity transmitters were disconnected and the companies reimbursed the telephone company for the estimated amount of the charges to avoid the scandal of prosecution. But there are undoubtedly many other computer systems that continue to enjoy free use of telephone lines.

BEEPERS

Ever since James Bond followed supercriminal Goldfinger around Europe with the aid of a "bumper beeper," the beeper-type devices have been multiplying in use. These are miniature transmitters which, instead of sending out voices, send out beeps. A bumper beeper can be attached with strong magnets to the bumper or body of an automobile in seconds. Tailing the car becomes very easy, since the tailer, equipped with a radio receiver, can keep as far as three or four miles from the beeper on the car and rely on the beeps to lead him. The tailer can gauge the direction in which the car under surveillance is going, the approximate speed at which it is travelling and the distance between the tailer and the subject car.

Bumper beepers carry their own battery power supply, good for several days. Or they may be connected to the auto's power system and continue to function indefinitely.

It is not uncommon for bumper beepers and voice bugs to be installed in new cars before they are delivered to customers—without the customer being told about it, of course. Automobile salesmen in the United States and many European countries have discovered that they can pick up extra money by tipping off certain investigation bureaus that they are delivering a new car to a celebrity or VIP. If a bureau is interested in following the activities of the customer in question they will pay the salesman well to have him install a beeper and a bug, and perhaps a tap on the radio-telephone if the car is equipped with one. Several leading politicians in Germany and France who bought new cars from a certain dealer in Düsseldorf in 1973 found that their vehicles came equipped with these unwanted accessories.

Some people who get as far as the German and French borders only to be arrested for attempting to smuggle dangerous drugs are genuinely confused. They seem unable to understand why the border police chose their car to search. In many cases they have been double-crossed by the dealers who sold them the drugs in another country. These drug dealers know that the police in many countries pay generous rewards for information leading to the arrest of drug smugglers. When selling drugs to a customer they manage to clip a magnet beeper to the customer's automobile. Later, the dealer telephones the police and gives the registration number of his customer's car. When the customer drives up to a border control station, the beep from the transmitter fastened to his car is picked up by a radio receiver in the station office. The police take the car apart and usually find hidden drugs. If an arrest follows, the dealer collects a reward—having already pocketed the proceeds from the sale of the drugs.

Another form of beeper is made up of thin components and a short strand of wire (the antenna). It has no power supply of its own, but it is sensitive to radiation from nearby transmitters and emits a beep when such transmitters are nearby. In order to activate one of these beepers, a transmitter or radio receiver must be within a hundred yards of the beeper. This means that in open country the tailer with his radio receiver must stay closer to the subject carrying the beeper, since the beeper is dependent upon radiation from the receiver. But in a town or city, where there are many transistor radios in use as well as car radios and radio-telephones, this kind of beeper can obtain its energy for many different sources, so that the tailer can keep farther in the background.

Such thin beeper devices can be laminated in credit cards, I.D. cards and even paper business cards. If the plastic or paper, between which the postage-stamp size beeper components and their antenna are sandwiched, is opaque, the presence of the beeper cannot be detected by holding the card up to a bright light.

A blackmailer, operating in Cannes during the Film Festival a year or two ago, got his information by handing celebrities his business card and then following the beeper with a receiver in his pocket. In this way he established who was sleeping with whom and this gave him the foundation for blackmail threats. When police searched his hotel room they found dozens of dossiers on film stars, directors, producers and promoters—all based in part on information he had obtained with the use of his beeper devices.

THE TECHNOLOGY OF HIDING BUGS

Radio bugs lend themselves to concealment within a wide range of everyday articles without arousing suspicion—coffee pots, table lamps, ashtrays, lighters, books, wastepaper baskets, electric extension cords and clocks. A meeting room in Brussels that was to be used for a top-secret conference had been thoroughly inspected by experts using special equipment as a safeguard against the use of concealed radio transmitters. All participants and attendants were then carefully searched before entering the room to make certain that no one carried a device in his pocket or brief case. Yet a full-length tape recording of the entire proceedings was made by a news service that bribed a waiter to carry their radio transmitter into the room. He, too, was searched as he carried a tray of coffee inside. When he finished serving there were several cups of coffee left on a side table. In the bottom of one, hidden by the coffee, was a "sugar cube microphone transmitter." It was sealed in a silicone shell to protect the parts from the liquid. Yet it picked up even whispered voices in the room and transmitted them clearly to a tape recorder in a news reporter's brief case in. the men's room 150 yards away.

Portable tape recorders worn in a pocket or shoulder holster can be attached to a variety of microphones disguised as tie clips, cufflinks, pens, watches, belt buckles, etc., which will pick up sounds up to twenty feet away. The same devices are also available in the form of microphone transmitters that will transmit everything being said around the person wearing them and send it to a radio receiver up to half a mile away.

The working ballpoint pen which contains a miniature microphone and broadcasting station is a handy device if you want to find out what people are saying behind your back. Suppose you are in a business meeting. Leave the pen, turned on, atop a desk or table and excuse yourself to go to the bathroom. Then, in the privacy of the bathroom, take a tiny FM radio—which you have conveniently brought along—from your pocket and tune it in to the frequency on which the pen is broadcasting. You can hear what the people are saying while you are out of the room.

The technology which makes possible these miniaturized wireless transmitters owes much to the NASA space and missile programs. Tape recordings of meetings of alleged Mafia leaders in a trailer in a New York City junkyard which led to their arrest and conviction were made with the aid of tiny microphone transmitters concealed in the ventilation ducts of the trailer. These devices, called Model T 1014DS, are high-band VHF (FM) transmitters which employ linear integrated circuits that were originally developed for fourth-generation computer systems.

If you think your telephone is bugged, it may be an unwarranted fear, but your hunch could prove valid. In most cases it takes only one phone call to bring a telephone company engineer with his sophisticated detecting devices to find out if there is a bug. Of course, if the police or some government agency has put a tap on your telephone for some reason, don't expect the engineer to tell you about it. Even though he may find a tap and remove it, it is quite likely you will never learn who was monitoring your telephone.

Sometimes people discover quite by accident that their telephone is being tapped:

A New York executive who drives home to Connecticut every evening used the cassette recorder in his automobile to record a special business news program broadcast over an FM station while he was enroute. It was his habit to play back the program the next morning on his way into town to brief him on the latest developments and the status of key stocks before he arrived at the office. One morning, as he listened to the tape, it was interrupted by the voice of his own daughter. She was talking on the telephone with a classmate comparing notes on school homework. How could this happen unless . . .?

Right. His home telephone was tapped with a microphone transmitter that just happened to cut into the frequency used by the FM radio station.

Another company official, this time in Turin, Italy, was in the habit of dictating important confidential memos to his secretary over the telephone on Saturday mornings as he lay in bed. A villain who was interested in finding out the contents of those memos put a tap on the secretary's telephone and fed the signal into a tape recorder. He was caught and convicted for installing and using an unlicensed radio transmitter for telephone tapping. His penalty: A $55 fine and $12 in court costs. No one bothered to disconnect the tap equipment, so he continued to use it. He was arrested a second time on the same charge. This conviction carried a penalty of $100 and $15 in court costs. The police took out the tap, but instead of confiscating it they returned it to the villain. He put it right back on the same telephone. But by then the official had abandoned giving dictation to his secretary on the telephone.

BUGS AND THE LAW

In the spring of 1974 several governments made new laws toughening the procedures controlling the use of wiretaps, bugging devices and secret recordings. All are aimed at excessive abuses of privacy.

Now anyone in Italy wishing to install an eavesdropping device or a recorder—such as an attaché case with a device carried into a board room to pick up a discussion during a meeting—must first obtain the permission of a magistrate. Otherwise such actions are illegal. The penalty is a term in prison of up to forty-eight months. The new law further provides that any compromising information—even that which reveals major criminal acts—which is obtained by illegal use of listening devices may not be used as evidence in the courts.

Italian magistrates are instructed not to accede to the installation of such surveillance equipment unless there is probable cause to believe that drug trafficking, counterfeiting or serious crimes of violence are involved.

Tape recordings of telephone conversations have been extensively used in recent months by Italian police in their war on the Mafia. The new law will allow them to continue to use wiretap recordings in drug, hijacking, art theft and murder cases, but if the case involves prostitution, blackmail, certain kinds of larceny and other so-called "lesser crimes" it will not be as easy as before to obtain authorization to install the tap.

Furthermore, if an authorized eavesdropping operation is carried out to obtain evidence in a murder case, and the eavesdroppers happen to listen in on information that can be used as evidence in bringing other kinds of charges the new law does not allow them to do so. Permission to eavesdrop is granted only for the investigation of previously specified charges.

Court-authorized wiretapping in the United States rose 43 percent in 1972 over the annual average of the previous ten years, according to Department of Justice figures (*New York Times*, May 6, 1973). "We are balancing off the right of privacy versus the need for better law enforcement," a spokesman for the department commented. This is a prefabricated statement that is held ready for release whenever there is the danger someone will point out that the fundamental right of every citizen to his privacy is being neglected.

The United States Supreme Court granted the wider use of evidence in a decision given on February 20, 1974. It held that evidence gathered through a legal (i.e., court-ordered) wiretap or bugging can be used against persons not specifically under surveillance.

Unlike the restriction imposed on police in Italy, U.S. law enforcement agencies no longer need investigate every possible person a wiretap or bugging might incriminate before asking for a warrant. The issue arose from a tap placed on the telephone of a man suspected of illegal gambling activities. After the wiretap was installed, the government sought to use evidence gathered by listening to the conversations of his wife. The court in Chicago, where the charge was first brought, threw out the evidence against the wife. The government appealed to the Supreme Court, and the decision was reversed.

The majority opinion of the Supreme Court said that it was sufficient that the warrant specified a search for evidence of illegal activity and that it implied a request to gather evidence on "others as yet unknown." A dissenting opinion was written by Justice William O. Douglas, who said: "Under today's decision a wiretap warrant apparently need specify only one name and a national dragnet becomes operative."

It is doubtful that the new laws and expanding of powers under existing laws will prevent the widespread abuses of telephone tapping as intended. The process of obtaining court orders is complicated by the overlapping jurisdictions of a multiplicity of law enforcement agencies in many countries. Nor do the new laws provide penalties for the mysterious disappearance of recordings or of conveniently erased or edited parts.

In some areas, where the law seems to fail to give prompt or adequate relief, technology may help. Laser, for example, holds promise for supplying protection against eavesdroppers.

Unlike cables and microwave links, a laser beam used for communications is difficult, if not impossible, to tap or bug. Its handicap is that it can only be used for point-to-point transmissions over relatively short distances. In time these disadvantages could be overcome. However, today's laser communications systems are impressive, and they have stumped the villains who would eavesdrop.

One installation in West Germany has been in operation for about two years continuously, through snow, smog, and the type of heavy interference which jams radio communications. It links three facilities of a major corporation—the executive offices, financial department and computer center, and manufacturing plant and warehouse. The distance between the first two is just over 1 kilometer, and each of them is approximately 2.5 kilometers from the manufacturing plant. Laser beams connect all three, like the legs of a triangle.

This laser system transmits and receives video, audio and computer data transmissions, handling corporate management information, stock control, data processing, visual material in color, facsimile reproduction of documents and a wide variety of other corporate information needs.

As we have seen, technology has made eavesdropping a boon to the electronic criminal—but it can also outwit him.

7

The Criminal Artist:
Fakes, Forgers
and Counterfeiters

During the summer of 1974 the Japanese had the bright idea of holding an art exhibition consisting entirely of fakes. They were Matisses and Modiglianis all painted by master forger Elmyr de Hory.

Forgery is an ancient art that today has been updated by the computer. The modern forger doesn't need to have the kind of talent exhibited by de Hory, who has been described by Clifford Irving in the de Hory biography *Fake* as probably the world's greatest art forger.

The majority of forgers have an interest in the kind of art that appears on banknotes, passports, stock certificates and other valuable pieces of paper. It has become so easy to make forgeries that many people who would not otherwise be tempted to try are now doing it. Photocopy machines are accessible to everybody—if you don't have one in your office there is the coin-operated machine at a railroad terminal or library.

Computers also make errors that invite forgery. In Oklahoma, the state computer accidentally generated sixteen duplicate automobile driving licenses and sent them to a man who had passed his driving test and was waiting for his license. This fellow obviously had larceny in his heart because he seized the opportunity to use the spare genuine licenses as identification when he cashed bad checks at stores and hotels. He removed his name from each of the fifteen spare license certificates and inserted false names. Then he signed each license so that the signature matched the false name. with these documents he went on an international check-cashing spree that netted him $160,000 in cash, goods and services before police, alerted by Interpol and the FBI, caught him in Barcelona.

An Interpol alert also resulted in the arrest of Antonio Constantini, an Italian thirty-nine years old, as he was enjoying a luxurious life aboard his boat *El Sol.* He had sailed into the port of Monte Carlo for the weekend on Friday, September 13, 1974.

On July 23, 1974, it is alleged that Constantini received 110 million Italian lira from a Swiss speculator in payment for forty-five ingots of "pure gold." The customer's greed for a bargain evidently made him overlook the normal precaution of having the gold examined. Later, when Constantini was far away spending his windfall, the customer claimed he discovered that he had bought *some* gold—but only a thin layer covering bars of lead.

According to friends of Constantini, he had found the "gold bars" in a warehouse where materials formerly used in window displays and exhibits were stored. He discovered that the coating on the lead was genuine gold. All that the bars needed to pass as bank gold were the markings. They claim he studied magazine photos of genuine gold ingots and did some other research on the subject to find the source of supply for dies with which to stamp the metal. It is said that with great care he applied the markings, then hunted for a "sucker" who would buy them. This was not difficult, because gold speculators were everywhere, ready to buy anything that appeared to be the real thing—coins, jewelry, ingots, even old fillings from teeth.

"He would never have done it if he had not come upon those dummy ingots," one of his friends claims. "Constantini was an honest man until the temptation came his way."

When the bubble burst for him in Monte Carlo, Constantini had only 35 million of the 110 million Italian lire left. The night before his arrest he slept under the stars on his boat. As this is written he is awaiting extradition in a palace without stars, the prison of Monaco.

A careless airline ticket agent is responsbile for giving a West German family an international first-class trip covering all of Europe. The family had planned to take an economy package tour to Portugal and were in the Düsseldorf air terminal waiting for their flight to Portugal. While they waited their eleven-year-old son made the rounds of various airline ticket counters, picking up schedules, brochures, and anything else that he found loose. Among other things he picked up eight blank passenger ticket coupon books and showed his collection to his parents.

The tickets had already been validated with a stamp and left behind on the counter by a clerk going off duty in preparation for a rush hour when many late arrivals would be coming in to buy their tickets. The spaces on the tickets for passenger's names and destinations were left blank.

The father seized the opportunity to give his family a better holiday. He cancelled their tour to Portugal and obtained a refund of the money he had paid. Then he filled in the blank tickets for Stockholm, Vienna, Rome, Cairo, Capetown and other cities he had always wanted to visit.

Seven months later the airline discovered it had given over 75,000 miles of free rides. It was then that the ticket coupons were processed in its accounting office.

If the agent in Düsseldorf had reported the loss of the tickets as soon as he discovered they were gone, the airline could have caught up with the family before they got very far. But the agent feared that his admission of carelessness would cost him his job, so he covered up.

Since the father used the family's true names in filling out the tickets, they were not difficult to trace. No criminal charges were made, but the airline has filed a suit for its money in civil court. It seems unlikely, however, that they will get relief. Many German courts, as well as those in other countries, have taken the view that, when the naivete or carelessness of an employee gives outsiders access to valuable company property, the employer cannot recover his losses. A sanitation truck worker in Munich who found a diamond brooch in a jewel box discarded in the trash by an employee of a jewelry shop was not obliged to pay when the shop owner sued him after he had sold the brooch.

Forgery and counterfeiting are also fertile fields for professional villains. Widespread interest in buying gold and silver coins and ingots as a hedge against inflation has spawned serious frauds among both amateur and professional crooks. Brokers and dealers, some with underworld connections, have been contracting to buy bags of silver and gold coins for investors. They take the investor's money but fail to buy the coins, using forged and counterfeit documents to cover up.

Louis Lefkowitz, Attorney General of the State of New York, alleged that brokers are defrauding tens of thousands of investors in various parts of the United States. The losses, he said on July 10, 1974, exceeded $200 million through just one "exchange" in the preceding year.

Mr. Lefkowitz alleged that one company's purchases were made of only enough silver coins to cover 1 to 15 percent of the orders it accepted. He claimed that investors were fraudulently advised the coins were being accumulated and held for them by means of forged bank vault receipts, and they they were also billed for storage charges with counterfeit invoices—and he obtained a court injunction barring the organization from doing business in New York.

Commenting on this action, a well-known expert in the money market, Nicholas Deak, said: "I believe that more silver coins have been sold than were ever produced before nickel-copper alloy replaced silver in American coinage in 1965."

Almost every type of document which represents

something of value has been forged or counterfeited at one time or another. When a breakfast cereal manufacturer offered to send the price of a box of strawberries (fifty cents) to anyone who mailed in three tops from boxes of his cornflakes, they received over 6,000 counterfeit box tops from addresses in the Chicago area. Clerks handling the transactions were found to have paid out nearly $500 in exchange for fake box tops before the fraud was discovered. The counterfeits were poorly done. Copies of genuine box tops were run off on a photocopy machine. These black-and-white copies were then pasted on strips of thin cardboard and mailed off for the money. One would have thought the clerks would have spotted the fakes immediately—but they did not.

THE BRITISH SAVINGS BOND FRAUD

A case involving British Post Office documents (Premium Bonds) is much more complex than counterfeiting box tops—and also more lucrative. According to testimony given in June 1972 at the trial in Old Bailey, the scheme originated with a postal telegraph officer who was the mastermind. It involved forging Premium Bonds in three fictitious names, making applications to cash them in on official forms, and forging the Post Office approval to allow the funds to be paid out. With the aid of accomplices employed by the Post Office, the telegraph officer was able to process the forged documents through internal channels and to be notified when the authority to pay out on the Premium Bonds had been received at branch post offices selected by the gang for collecting the money.

In a single day the gang collected over $275,000 by cashing forged bonds at 133 post offices in the greater London area. In addition, they got away with more than $80,000 using other forged Post Office documents. "Got away" is perhaps a misleading phrase, however, for all were finally caught.

One of the accomplices, a forty-five-year-old exconvict who learned the art of forgery in prison, appeared as chief prosecution witness after aiding detectives in their inquiries. From the villain's viewpoint he was the weak link in the scheme. He knew enough to put everyone (except himself) behind bars—and that is exactly what he did.

In such cases, investigators hammer away at suspected members of a gang until one of them starts talking. The larger the gang, the easier the case is to solve, generally speaking. The Premium Bond gang failed, perhaps, because there were too many accomplices.

FORGERY BY THE BOOK

"It is unfortunate that details such as this should have been given in a book." This comment, by a British judge, on February 22, 1974, focuses attention on the fact that honest people sometimes do turn to crime as the result of reading a novel, watching a movie or picking up information from other mass media sources.

The judge was referring to a twenty-three-year-old secretary who used the method of obtaining false passports described by novelist Frederick Forsyth in his thriller *The Day of the Jackal.*

After reading the book, the secretary found the names of dead people and visited three Registry Offices in the London area. Upon payment of the fee—and claiming that she had a legitimate right to make the application— she obtained copies of birth certificates for these dead people. She then used the certificates as proof of identity to obtain genuine passports which bore the deceased person's name and particulars. She used her own photograph and forged the deceased person's name. In selecting the dead people to impersonate, she followed advice given in the novel to pick subjects of her own age, race, and origins.

Why did this secretary do this? The police were not looking for her; she had no bill collectors on her trail. But her employer was in serious trouble with the law, with his wife, and with creditors. He decided to leave England and assume a new identity in South Africa. He asked her to accompany him, which she agreed to do. But, obviously, if she used her own passport and true name he could have been traced through her.

Having read the method explained in *The Day of the Jackal*, she followed the instructions and did it herself, obtaining not one new identity but a pair of spares in case of future need.

When her employer's false identity was uncovered in South Africa, however, she too was arrested and returned to England. In court, her attorney pointed out that there was no question of her being involved in her employer's criminal activities and that the series of events had been a "most shattering experience for her." The judge took this into consideration along with a report from the Fraud Squad that she had given them considerable help, and fined her $750.

This is by no means an isolated case. Implicit in every story of a crime is the potential for encouraging dishonesty. Even when the villains are caught, there may be a reader who thinks he is smarter than those villains—and he may be tempted to repeat the *modus operandi* and profit from their mistakes.

A SHOWER OF PHONY DOLLARS OVER ROME

A few years ago an enterprising movie producer promoted his new film about a bank robbery by dropping thousands of fake United States $1 banknotes from a helicopter over the streets of Rome and other Italian cities. The backside of the papers carried an advertisement for the film, but the face was a very good reproduction of a genuine one-dollar bill—with one exception. Instead of the face of George Washington was a picture of the star of the movie.

Astonishingly enough, several dozen of these fake banknotes were accepted as legal tender by clerks in shops where tourists often bought souvenirs with American money. There were also cases in which clerks caught the fakes and called in the police to arrest the passer. Newspapers wrote amusing stories about how people had been fooled and gave much free publicity to the movie.

One journalist, a specialist in satire, published an article in which he described how a fictional villain had picked up several piles of the fake banknotes, tied them in bundles with a few genuine $1 bills on top, and exchanged them for lire at currency exchange bureaus. The writer pointed out that the ends of the face side of the fakes looked very real and that cashiers saw the genuine bills on top and then counted the fakes along with them without unwrapping the bundles. In this way they failed to see the movie star's picture in the center.

Within a week after this essay appeared, three currency exchange bureaus in Italy accepted packets of money that were later found to contain only five genuine one-dollar bills and ninety-five fakes—and gave good lire for them. A warning notice about this swindle was circulated to banks and money changing offices. But this failed to stop cashiers from being taken in. Swindlers managed to pass off nearly twenty more packets before they gave up, their supply of the advertising bills having been exhausted, or the risk having become so great it seemed no longer worth taking.

Police believe that this swindle was not the work of professionals—the rewards were not big enough for them. It was probably done by a number of people who simply took advantage of an opportunity.

The movie producer, who was indirectly responsible for the "crime wave," paid restitution to the money exchange offices. After all, he gained a million dollars' worth of free publicity.

SCOPE OF THE CRIMES

If this Italian incident seems incredible, we can find numerous other cases in which the public has been fooled by counterfeit and forged documents. In 1819 an English forger made one-pound notes on ordinary white paper with pen and ink. They proved irresistible to a great mass of the population. Articles about his success encouraged others to try their hand. By 1827, 94,000 persons had been arrested in England for the crime of forgery. So serious did the problem become that Parliament instituted the death penalty for this offense. Over 7,500 of those arrested during this period were executed.

At present, forgery and counterfeiting crimes are growing at a steady rate. In early 1974 the British Law Commission put together a workmanlike report recommending revisions in the penal codes on Forgery and Counterfeiting Currency, an indication that it is still an important concern in English life. Similar studies are being undertaken in other countries.

At best, any statistics on the total annual losses through fraudulent documents in any given country can only be qualified estimates projected from the results of limited surveys. Published estimates of the losses in the United States range from $70 million (American Bankers Association) to $1 billion (Better Business Bureau). A compilation of data in the Common Market countries of Europe, before Britain joined, indicates annual losses in the neighborhood of $400 million. Britain alone, at this same time, was said to have reported losses from forgery and counterfeiting of about $15 million.

Between 1960 and 1970 forged bank checks accounted for about 70 percent of all kinds of forgeries. Passports, prescriptions, wills, stock and bond certificates and other documents took care of the rest. Since 1970, however, there has been a sharp rise in these other types of documents. More medical prescriptions are being forged by drug users; passport forgeries are encountered more frequently; and so on. Today, in 1975, forged bank checks probably account for less than 50 percent of the total; the gap is made up by fraudulent credit cards (which are easier to use than checks) and other kinds of documents.

A study* of 500 persons convicted of forgery and

*From a study made by the State of California Department of Corrections with the cooperation of the Federal Bureau of Prisons.

counterfeiting crimes reveals that 70 percent of them have two distinguishing characteristics:

1. A degree of clerical skill and at least an elementary business knowledge.

2. An exceptional amount of the type of courage which is sometimes called "guts."

In this group were people of both sexes, young and old, and of all races. An elderly Chinese woman was a professional check passer. She hauled in over $30,000 a year for twelve years before she was caught. These people were all convicted of the crimes; the study tells us nothing about those who get away with it, because the villains who are successful remain anonymous. They can be presumed to have these additional distinguishing characteristics:

3. "Honest" appearance, apparent good character and respectable dress.

4. Ability to answer test questions which people who regularly cash checks sometimes ask.

Some types of forgery are carried out by "loners," and others are carried out by gangs or rings.

THE MULTIMILLION-DOLLAR CHECK-PASSING RING AND ITS CODE OF TERROR

VICTIMS: Banks, retail stores, transportation companies, automobile dealers, others who cash or accept checks.

VILLAINS: Organized forgery ring, operating internationally in many cases. Some rings number over 200 people. As this is written, such rings are known to be operating with headquarters in Nice, France; London; Coral Gables, Florida; Honolulu; East Berlin; and Tel Aviv, Israel. These rings have branch operations in principal cities throughout the world.

PLOT: The operating forgery ring has several functions: (a) buying stolen travellers' checks, checkbooks with check cashing cards, credit cards, and identity documents (passports, driver's licenses, etc.) from petty thieves, pickpockets, and dishonest hotel employees in busy tourist centers; (b) altering the documents to make them suitable for use by people who negotiate the checks and credit cards (changing pictures on passports, applying appropriate official government stamps, etc.); and (c) cashing the checks, by persons with no previous criminal records who are perhaps in financial difficulties and who are willing to be recruited as "passers." A productive forged check ring can average a net income of $100,000 a day with one hundred passers or "collectors."

Almost daily, parcels containing bundles of newly stolen checks, credit cards and identity documents arrive by air at Nice Airport. Speed is essential, for the success of a forgery ring depends on getting these documents and checks altered and into the hands of passers before their loss is reported by the owners and warning notices are sent out to banks, shops, airlines, etc. At best, a forgery ring cannot count on more than fifteen days before documents become too risky to pass. With some documents, like American Express and Barclay's travellers' checks, the safe period is less than one week—and with computer-assisted warning systems the time is becoming even shorter.

Parcels of stolen documents are picked up at the airport by messengers and quickly dispatched to "processing centers" where professional forgers with all the necessary equipment make the necessary alterations. Many of the parcels arriving at Nice from far-distant cities in North America, Europe and Africa, with which it has direct flight connections, are carried by car over the Autoroute to a processing center in Italy, not far from Savona. There "passer's kits" are made up. Using I.D. photos of passers already working with the ring, the forgers exchange pictures on identity documents, insert fake official stamps and perform whatever operations are needed to make up a kit which allows the passer to identify himself as the legitimate owner of the checks or other negotiable papers.

The passer's kits are then sent off quickly to people whose job it is to supervise a team of passers. From Savona, for example, the kits are carried by car to the airport at Geneva, Switzerland—because Italian mail services are so unreliable. Mailed from there to distributors around the world, kits can be placed in the hands of passers in no less than ninety-six hours after the original documents have been stolen. This gives the passer no more than two or three days to negotiate the checks before he runs the risk of being caught.

Passers are often recruited through newspaper ads offering the opportunity to make high commissions as salesmen without previous experience ($100 a day guaranteed) or offering unsecured loans at modest interest rates. Other passers are recruited by hotel employees, who often meet people who have run out of funds while travelling. Careful background checks are run on candidates. Those who are accepted learn that they will negotiate checks and turn the proceeds over to the ring's distributor, keeping 10 percent of the gross for this service. Each passer is given a daily gross quota—$200 for a beginner, $1,000 for an experienced passer. Most rings do not allow their passers to work more than three days in a given city. Some rings fly their passers into a city in a group in the morning. They split up and spend the day negotiating forged paper, and then meet at the airport to take a late evening flight out of town. This is an expensive operation, but the profits are very high.

A forged travellers' check ring under scrutiny by Scotland Yard is alleged to have made a profit in excess of £6 million in 1972. This ring has thus far evaded detection.

A forgery ring's "carve-up threat" sealed the lips of Robert Buckley, a passer who was arrested in England. Buckley risked trying to pass some forged travellers' checks that were "too old" and lost. He was taken into custody at Heathrow Airport on September 16, 1973, after a cashier at Lloyd's Bank Money Enchange recognized that the numbers of the checks he presented were on the hot list. Detectives asked Buckley for the names of other members of his ring.

"You must be joking," he told them. He refused to name the men in the forgery ring because they had threatened to "carve up" his attractive common-law wife if he ever talked. His defense lawyer, Mr. Richard

Haworth, confirmed that Buckley was informed "by some source that if he gave names away harm would come to his wife." Such codes of terror are common in forgery rings.

Buckley, a thirty-two-year-old former jockey (who had to give it up because he got too heavy) and nightclub croupier, admitted passing twenty American Express travellers' checks known to him to have been stolen; receiving a stolen passport; and being an accessory in the forgery of a passport. He also admitted to forging travellers' checks at three London airport banks.

When he appeared for sentencing at the Old Bailey on July 3, 1974, the judge postponed fixing his prison term in the hope that he could be persuaded to give evidence that would enable Scotland Yard to break up the ring.

Not all check forgers belong to rings. Working alone some of these people have very quickly taken in tens of thousands of dollars.

THE METHODS OF THE LONE CHECK FORGER

As with the member of a forgery ring, the loner must obtain blank check forms, travellers' checks or checks already made out to another person to which he needs only add an endorsement. He must also supply himself with identity papers to support the names he uses on the checks.

Blank check forms with the name of a local bank are sometimes found on counters in business firms for the convenience of customers, particularly in smaller towns. Blank checks may also be purchased at stationery and office supply stores, but these require the name of the bank and account number to be filled in. Unless the user is known, such checks are difficult to negotiate. There are also numerous cases in which villains have visited printing plants that do forms for banks. Representing themselves as employees of a new bank planning to open a branch in the city, they ask for samples of the work they have done for other bank customers—deposit slips, credit memos, and (naturally) checks. Printers have been known to give "prospective customers" whole books of checks as samples of their product.

More commonly, the forger will steal checkbooks from an office. Company check blanks are very desirable, because they are easy to negotiate. Posing as a window cleaner, decorator or salesman, the villain will wait for the chance to tear a number of checks from the back of a book that someone has carelessly left unattended. Sometimes villains go directly to banks to steal checks.

Over a period of three years a painter and handyman financed trips through England, Ireland and Europe. He wound up entering a plea of guilty in the Old Bailey courts in London in September 1972.

In his confession, John Roche said it all started when he obtained a job as a painter to redecorate the Elephant and Castle branch of Lloyd's Bank. He stole twenty-one checkbooks which the staff did not bother to lock up. He next got work at the Midland Bank's Knightsbridge branch, where he walked out with seventy-three checkbooks. Soon after, he persuaded an employee of the Muswell Hill branch of Lloyd's Bank to let him in after hours to make an estimate for a painting job. There he got away with only nine checkbooks.

Roche sold some of the checkbooks to friends, who paid him as much as $250 for a book of thirty checks. He used the others to finance his trips.

"I found it far less risky to get postal orders instead of passing checks at banks or business places," he told police. By this technique he turned forged checks into $58,000 in cash. In addition, he hired six cars from rent-a-car agencies, drove them abroad via car ferry boats and sold them to raise an additional $30,000.

After he was sentenced to prison for four years, Roche made an interesting statement: "It's still better than printing your own money," he said. "The penalty for counterfeiting is much stiffer."

Roche established his identity, or false identity, by using check cashing cards which he stole from the banks at the same time he took the blank checks.

Identification papers are necessary for the forger. Documents such as identity cards, Social Security cards, driver's licenses, credit cards, and bank check cashing cards are usually accepted by people who cash checks. Of course, a passport, even a bogus one, is the best identification.

In 1973 a professional forger visited the Automobile Association offices at Leicester Square in London to buy some road maps. While there he noticed a stack of blank International Driving Permits on a receptionist's desk. When she was not looking, he pocketed a handful. These documents, issued by the auto club for the British Ministry of Transport are recognized throughout the world. All he needed to do was to fill one out whenever he needed an identity to match the name on some checks, attach a picture of himself (taken in an automatic photo machine), and add the impression of the letters AA with a home rubber stamp printing outfit. With this identification he passed 300 checks in two days at banks in Belgium, Holland and France for a total of over $8,000. Speed was the main ingredient of his success, as it is in most check-passing schemes.

If the check passer moves quickly he does not allow enough time for the check casher to verify whether or not the check is good (and, if it is not, to call the police). The passer also cuts the time for negotiating a check by not writing it for a large amount. British forgers usually ask for no more than between twenty or thirty pounds. The average fraudulent check negotiated in the United States is about eighty dollars. In France the average is 300 francs, and in Germany it is 165 marks.

THE "IMMEDIATE CASH" FRAUD

VICTIMS: The bank—and the person whose signature has been forged.

VILLAIN: Professional forger.

PLOT: The forger opens an account at a bank in order to become a legitimate customer. The initial deposit is small, but he tells the bank he is expecting a substantial sum. A few days later he presents a worthless check, usually drawn against the account of a well-known corporation in a foreign country. With it, he presents a deposit slip and tells the cashier he wants part of the proceeds of his check credited to his account and the balance in cash.

In one recent case, a forger presented a check for $10,540 drawn on IBM's account in New York at the Paris branch of a U.S. bank where he had just opened an account. He had stamped the check CERTIFIED and initialed the certification. He asked for $3,200 in cash— and he got it. It took two weeks for the check to be cleared and the Paris bank to learn of its loss.

THE "MAY I MAKE IT FOR A LITTLE EXTRA" FRAUD

VICTIMS: Retail establishments which sell at high prices.

VILLAIN: Friendly, intelligent and respectable-looking forger.

PLOT: Harry Haines, born in Moundsville, West Virginia, was a master check passer. He successfully pursued his forgery career for fifty years and toured the world several times on the proceeds of bad checks. He never spent a night in jail, except one when he was put in a drunk tank for being disorderly—he urinated on a police car while under the influence of too many bourbons. The key to his success was that he limited his take from each transaction to a small sum, never more than thirty dollars. According to the history on file at the John Jay College of Criminal Justice, Haines's method consisted of going into a store which sold expensive items like photographic equipment, antiques, jewelry, tableware and china, and into art galleries. He carefully selected and purchased several hundred dollars' worth of goods, saying that he wanted to pay for them but would pick them up at a later time or have them delivered to a fictitious address. When he started to write the check, Haines casually would ask the clerk: "Do you mind if I make it for a little extra? I've been doing a lot of shopping and I'm short of pocket money." Almost invariably the clerk—already occupied with figuring up his own commission on the sale—would agree to this. He received his receipt and the twenty or thirty dollars in change. Then he walked out of the store never to be seen again. In this way he hauled in $90 to $150 in an average working day. Harry Haines's luggage included a complete outfit for practicing his trade: a printing press for manufacturing checks with the names and logotypes of well-known banks: Bank of America, First National City Bank, Barclays, Société Générale, and some fictitious banks that never existed, like the Andrew Carnegie Trust Company and the American Fidelity Bank of Illinois. He also carried a variety of identity papers and fake letters of introduction from leading corporations (since he often posed as a travelling representative of these firms). A careful man, Haines put all of his proceeds into travellers' checks. When he died in Miami, Florida, of a heart attack, at age seventy-one, some $17,000 in travellers' checks were found among his effects, along with an account book listing the places he had visited and the stores he had victimized for eleven years prior to his death. It was clear that he never visited the same firm twice. Like many of the most successful forgers, Haines was a loner—but he was not alone at the game. Police records in every major city show that Haines's *modus operandi* continues to be used by many with considerable success.

Fraud and forgeries are by no means limited to the prosperous countries, like the United States and those in Western Europe. Villains have already gained a foothold in the "developing nations," bringing with them their latest schemes. The absence of legal restraints against fraud in many such places makes them attractive targets. Barclay's Bank of Zambia, Ltd., held a two-day briefing for law enforcement officers and businessmen in 1973 after the villains moved in.

THE BOGUS SECURITY OFFICER FRAUD

VICTIMS: Retail stores of large size, and customers.

VILLAIN: A crook posing as a store security officer, often wearing a store badge.

PLOT: The villain strolls among shoppers until he spots one paying for her purchase by check. He then approaches the customer and introduces himself as a security officer. He explains that the store has taken in some bad checks and asks to examine the checkbook and any identification papers that the customer may have. This sounds quite normal, and the customer suspects nothing even when the security man excuses himself to take the checkbook and I.D. papers to "the office" for verification. By the time the customer and the clerk become alarmed because he has not returned, the bogus security officer has left the store and passed the checkbook and I.D. to a confederate who is an expert at copying handwriting and signatures. The confederate works speedily, so that even while the customer is explaining what has happened to a genuine store official, checks are being negotiated in another store nearby. A single team of fraudsmen raked in $8,000 using this trick in three days in Zambia. They disappeared before police machinery could be set in motion to catch them.

THE DUAL SIGNATURE FRAUD

One of the most accomplished forgers of our times, and a man whose methods have been widely copied, was a New Yorker, Alexander Thiel. In three years, during World War II, he obtained $250,000 by his own estimate. Police suspect that his actual take was at least double that amount because the victims declined prosecution due to fear of adverse publicity.

Thiel broke into business offices to obtain his blank checks. After removing checks from a book he would write on the stubs: "VOID, ERROR," or "CHECK REMOVED, DEFECTIVE PRINTING." If a company check-writing machine was available he would use it to stamp the amounts of the check and authorizing signatures to give greater authenticity to his bogus paper.

Next, Thiel would burglarize the office of a second executive—the man whose name he planned to use in forging the checks. He would take away with him business letterheads and envelopes, correspondence addressed to the man and canceled checks or other documents containing his signature.

Armed with these papers he would go to a bank and open an account in the name of the executive—pretending to be that man. Using one of the stolen checks, already made out to this man for several thousand dollars, he made an initial deposit.

Thiel would then test both the office where he stole the checks and the man whom he was impersonating at the bank. In a telephone call to the bookkeeper at the office he would ask questions that would cause the bookkeeper to examine the checkbook. If the bookkeeper noticed the removed checks he would probably communicate his concern over the irregularity to Thiel. Next he called the man he was impersonating. Pretending to be an official of the bank where he had opened the account who was soliciting business. If the bank had already contacted the executive to verify that he had opened the account, the man would surely comment on it. If the results of these two inquiries reassured Thiel that all was well, he went ahead with the next step.

Allowing time for the large deposited check to clear through the bank on which it was drawn, he then started making substantial withdrawals, using his assumed identity. Before the bookkeeper received his monthly bank statement, Thiel cashed all the checks on the account that he wanted.

Thiel's success was founded in his remarkable penmanship. He could reproduce a signature easily after practicing only one or two times. He also did his homework so that he could give authentic references when he opened an account. He was able to give as reference the bank in which the executive he was impersonating actually had an account. Furthermore, he forged the man's signature on a signature card in the presence of a bank officer. This signature would be forwarded to the reference bank, which declared it genuine.

One of the executives Thiel impersonated was a stockbroker, Bertram Campbell. He was suspected of perpetrating the fraud committed by Thiel, and in due course he was arrested. The circumstantial evidence was so strong against him, particularly since both he and Thiel wore small mustaches which eyewitnesses remembered, that he was convicted. Campbell was completely innocent, yet he served three years in prison before Thiel was arrested in another matter and in the course of interrogation confessed to the fraud. Campbell was released and exonerated, but nothing could compensate him for the miscarriage of justice that put him behind bars for over thirty-six months.

Statistics show that check frauds dominate the field of crimes against property. Yet in many countries there are no laws which specifically prohibit this type of offense. The French Penal Code is an exception. It makes the passing of a bad check a crime, subject only to the general defense that it was issued in good faith. The Penal Codes in some American states also cover "insufficient funds" checks in addition to clear forgeries, so that a person who uses his own name can be prosecuted for passing a bad check. But in most of the rest of the world fraudulent check crimes are dealt with under a blanket or omnibus law which provides penalties for obtaining money or "pecuniary advantages" by deception. These laws are so obscurely worded that judges and jurors are sometimes overwhelmed when they attempt to apply them to particular acts.

The problem is that such existing laws are difficult if not impossible to adapt to the rapid changes in the nature of our money system. New practices like computer-based accounting systems to replace ledgers, check guarantee cards to replace personal credit worthiness and the expansion of banking and commercial enterprises beyond national borders are daily making loopholes in the law that are sufficient to let legions of villains operate with little risk of punishment. A single set of general legal principles about the protection of property is no longer adequate.

BOGUS BANKNOTES

On April 13, 1973, Dutch police raided a printing plant in a pension at Warmonderweg in Oegstgeest and found stacks of phony United States dollars—in denominations of ten, twenty, fifty and one hundred. The haul was valued at over eighteen million Dutch guilders. The printers and operators of the clandestine counterfeiting plant had vanished. Investigations revealed that they were probably the same counterfeiters who got away with their plates minutes before Paris police broke into a printing plant there on June 9, 1972. Police arrested several "retailers" of the bogus dollars, who had been paying the printers for them at the rate of one franc to the dollar. It is impossible to tell how much money this plant had put into circulation, but it had been operating for more than a year.

Another raid, also on June 9, 1972, by Turin, Italy, detectives netted three counterfeiters who are suspected of producing more than $4 million in "queer" Italian lire. During 1972 and 1973 there were seventy-four raids of this type in the Common Market countries. The banknotes found in many of them appear to be printed from plates made by one master engraver, according to Interpol's fake-banknote experts. They also traced the source of the watermarked papers used on printing both the fake dollars and lire to a papermill in Japan, which markets their products for legitimate uses in making stock certificates, bonds and college diplomas.

"The notes are nearly perfect," one investigator told me. "It is very difficult to identify it as counterfeit money."

Italian bank clerks accepted some of the fake lire as legal tender. More than $130,000 worth was found to be in circulation in banks.

THE MONEY FARM

In 1971, detectives raided an isolated Lincolnshire farmhouse and found a "veritable counterfeiter's den" complete with modern lithograph press, high-speed paper-cutting machine, Japanese watermarked paper, and 1,000 five-pound notes. If they had arrived a few hours earlier they could have stopped the shipment of several thousands more.

Two weeks later, police swooped on a house in Ilford, Essex, and found 13,000 more five-pound notes, part of the shipment they had missed. The next day, 20,000 more banknotes from the same Lincolnshire printing press were seized by Dutch police in Amsterdam.

In all, the police confiscated less than 40,000 fivers from Lincolnshire, but Interpol estimates that at least a million more were put into circulation. Thousands of them turned up in Australia, Canada, Malta, the Bahamas, and the United States, and were eventually recorded in Interpol files.

This world counterfeiting center first opened for business in London. But it attracted too much attention, and—one jump ahead of Scotland Yard—the villains shifted to the Linconlshire farmhouse. The printers were professionals who worked at regular, well-paying jobs during the week—but on Saturdays they went to spend a day in the country. In an eight-hour shift these operators turned out 192,000 bogus five-pound banknotes, four to a sheet at the rate of 6,000 sheets an hour.

They had no direct involvement in the distribution of the currency—few printers do. Once the sheets were chopped into separate notes by a paper cutter and packed in bundles of a hundred, they were sold to "wholesalers" who in turn sold the bogus currency to distributors in at least a dozen countries. Next they were sold to retailers. In this way a retailer has no direct contact with either the wholesaler or the printer. This makes for better security in the event of a police investigation.

Another world counterfeiting center was also discovered at Bromley, Kent, in the summer of 1973. The counterfeiting paraphernalia was even more up-to-date than that found at the farmhouse, and there was an engraving and die-making shop to prepare plates and consecutive numbering stamps for the fake banknotes. In addition, police found a laboratory for the analysis and comparison of genuine banknotes, with high-powered microscopes, chemical analysis equipment and hardware to study and apply coded magnetic stripes to notes of the type being used in several countries to facilitate counting and use of paper money in vending machines. There was even an embosser to be used in manufacturing fake Dutch guilders, which now feature a Braille code that enables the blind to identify the denomination of a note.

The stock on hand at the Bromley den included more than 1,000 U.S. fifty-dollar bills; 15,000 U.S. one-dollar bills; 2,000 Irish five-pound notes and an experimental run of British twenty-pound notes.

United States currency is by far the most popular with counterfeiters because it is easy to pass almost anywhere.

TRACING BOGUS BANKNOTES

Counterfeiting printing centers often go undetected for years. One in Hoboken, New Jersey, kept going for nineteen years, although dozens of people who were caught passing its fake currency were arrested. The police have learned to be very patient, and tipoffs about these operations come from unexpected places. A Philadelphia plant was uncovered as a result of a wife's cheating on her husband. Local police were conducting a campaign to track down "scofflaws." Among them was an owner of a Buick who had accumulated over $1,200 in unpaid parking tickets. He was sent a bill by the Traffic Violations Bureau. He demanded to see the copies of the citations.

All of the citations were issued during weekday hours when he was at his office, and all were for illegal parking in an area of the city he never visited. The only explanation was that his wife was using the family car without telling him.

He arranged to have her followed, and found out the address she visited regularly twice a week. It was a bookshop on a busy, noisy shopping street. When he confronted his wife with the evidence she admitted she was having an affair with the owner of the bookshop. Furthermore, she told him, her lover had a "money machine" in the basement. She showed him a fifty-dollar banknote she had taken as a souvenir.

The man went to the police and offered them a deal. If they would forget about his wife's parking violations he would lead them to a counterfeiting plant. He showed them the fifty-dollar bill. Detectives immediately recognized it as the product of a printer they had been hunting for nearly a decade. They accepted the offer.

Although the information he gave led to the arrest and conviction of the counterfeiter, police protected the identity of both the informant and his wife—and with good reason. This counterfeiting operation belonged to a powerful Cosa Nostra underworld "family."

Sometimes it is the counterfeiter himself who, by his own foolishness, gives himself away. This is how the Dutch police were led to the Oegstgeest plant in a 1973 case. One of the printers went to an Amsterdam supplier looking for the kind of watermarked paper they needed to print banknotes.

He was shown several sample sheets, including some imported from Japan. Then he made his fatal mistake. He took a stack of U.S. one-dollar bills from his pocket and laid them out in rows on the blank sheet of printing paper in order to see how many banknotes could be printed on one sheet. An observant salesman saw this, and after the counterfeiter left he reported the incident to the police. The matter was turned over to the Dutch State Police.

They put the customer under surveillance and within a few days confirmed that there was a counterfeiting center at Oegstgeest. They also identified several of the customer's associates, one of whom was a skilled engraver. The police could have raided the plant immediately, but they waited until after the order of watermarked printing paper was delivered and the plant was in full production. In this way they were able to seize as evidence the eighteen million guilders' worth of U.S. false banknotes. Unfortunately, they failed to capture any of the counterfeiters, even though they knew who they were. Whether they had been warned of the raid in time to flee the country, or whether by luck they just happened to be elsewhere and did not return after news of the raid was published in the newspapers, no one knows. However, several passers of fake banknotes did show up to replenish their supplies, and these people were arrested. However, the Dutch State Police were satisfied that they had prevented thousands of phony banknotes from being circulated.

Usually police are not so lucky. The conventional counterfeiting investigation begins with the discovery of some false notes in circulation, which police try to trace back to their source. This may take months, even years, and often ends in drawing a blank. Sometimes the counterfeiters have shut up shop by the time they are identified.

Such was the case with another clandestine printing plant in Holland a few years ago. Queer money which was spotted by bank clerks and shopkeepers on five continents was laboriously traced during sixteen months of inquiries to a printing operation near Haarlem. Police spent a small fortune on paid informants to obtain the address of the plant. When they finally got it and sent out a team of detectives to mount a stakeout to keep the place under surveillance, the detectives came back almost at once. The building where the plant had been was torn down to make way for a new shopping center.

There is excellent cooperation between international police, Interpol and law enforcement agencies in most countries for the apprehension of counterfeiters, because unchecked counterfeiting could bring about the collapse of national and world economies. It is much better cooperation than that given in investigating other types of con men.

Statistics about counterfeiting, as with other kinds of crime, are not reliable if an attempt is made to get an international estimate. But there are suitable indicators of the growth of the business of bogus banknotes in the last thirty years. In 1945 U.S. federal prisons had forty-seven counterfeiters in custody. In 1972 the number had increased to 506. On the other side of the Atlantic, the total number of arrests on counterfeiting charges—including passing fake money—in the United Kingdom, France, Germany, Benelux, Switzerland and Italy numbered slightly more than 40,000. In 1973 the statistics for these same countries had more than tripled. Much of this increase was due not only to a stepping up of traffic in bogus bills as the result of mounting inflation but also due to increased vigilance by law enforcement organizations and particularly police at border control stations.

The printing of counterfeit banknotes is not the only business of these villains. Some of them have turned to making other forms of fake paper that can be easily converted into genuine cash—stock certificates, for example.

FAKE SHARES MASK THEFTS

In 1966 Dr. Emil Savundra of Fire, Auto and Marine Insurance Company invested premium receipts in shares of Beaverbrook Newspapers, Burmah Oil, Simon Engineering, Great Universal Stores, Distillers and other good investments. The stock certificates were in the insurance company's vault in Zurich. The firm's auditors inspected them and were satisfied. It was not until someone checked with the registrars of the various firms who issued the shares that false serial numbers showed up and they were declared counterfeits. Dr. Savundra had used the fake shares to disguise his manipulations and thefts of $2,110,000 of the firm's money.

But he was not charged with counterfeiting. He went to jail because he stayed around until the insurance company went bankrupt and he was charged with criminal conspiracy to bring about its downfall.

For all anyone knows, Dr. Savundra's fraud is being repeated all over the world.

FRAUDULENT HEALTH CERTIFICATES

If there is enough money in it, a counterfeiter will even risk causing a world epidemic of a deadly disease. During a recent smallpox scare in Western Europe, Britain and other countries required all persons arriving from epidemic areas to produce health certificates. Counterfeiters in those places quickly took advantage of the situation and offered travellers bogus immunization records and forged stamps indicating that the bearer had recently been vaccinated against smallpox. Police at British ports of entry picked up dozens of these fake health documents, but many more probably slipped by. Fortunately, the disease did not erupt in Britain, but it easily could have. A printing plant where these documents were produced—in Bangladesh, where 1,000 died of smallpox—was raided, and 50,000 fake health certificates were found. These were genuine World Health Organization forms with forged vaccination certification and stamps. The buyer could fill in his own name. During the epidemic in 1973, the counterfeiters sold such cards at twelve to twenty dollars each.

BOGUS AIRLINE TICKETS

It is unlikely that there is a single international airline which has not had its tickets counterfeited at one time or another. The International Air Transport Association (IATA) estimates the losses to its members, including Pan Am, Air France, KLM, BOAC, Japan Airlines, and most of the other major scheduled air carriers, was more than $100 million in 1973.

"The financial troubles of many airlines are being seriously increased by the losses from counterfeiting," an IATA spokesman said. "We know of one carrier whose entire profits were wiped out in 1972 by bogus tickets."

IATA member airlines all use passenger ticket forms which conform to a standard format and are printed in several colors with carbon coating on the backside to facilitate making copies. These color shadings and the carbon coating are intended also to make counterfeiting more difficult.

Easier than a passenger ticket to counterfeit is another IATA form: the Miscellaneous Charges Order (MCO). This is a document issued to a passenger in lieu of a cash refund when he turns in an unused ticket. For practical purposes, it is a credit slip with a value up to $280 which will be honored by any IATA member airline as payment for tickets. The MCO's format resembles a passenger ticket; it does not have the same security protection in its printing, however, and therefore it is easier to simulate. As with tickets, it takes a long time for bogus MCO forms to be discovered because they, too, are fed into computers. As in all types of crime, the longer the interval between the crime and its discovery the less chance there is of catching the villain.

Counterfeiters are already robbing the world securities markets of astronomic sums. Nobody has been able to assess the dollar value of losses to investors, banks and investment firms as well as the corporations whose shares were faked. Senator John L. McClellan, Chairman of the U.S. Senate Permanent Subcommittee on Investigations, said in August 1971: "There are literally hundreds of thousands of people involved in swindles involving worthless and counterfeit securities."

This is a relatively new enterprise for counterfeiters. "It's the biggest opportunity we've ever had," said a Mafia-connected dealer in bogus shares in an interview with journalist Gay Talese in 1959. Since then the opportunities have increased a hundredfold.

8

The Money Machine,
Irma la Douce
and a Furnace Fraud

S ome otherwise honest business executives have been
carefully examining the methods used in classic
frauds and swindles to find out if they can be operated as
legitimate enterprises within the law, or in ways that
substantially reduce the risks of prosecution. The particular swindles that are of greatest interest are those which
have successfully accumulated colossal fortunes for the
villains involved.

One of these frauds is pyramid selling, which is the
biggest get-rich-quick swindle of all time and has been
called "the money machine" by some con men.

PYRAMID SELLING

VICTIMS: Anyone strongly motivated by greed.

VILLAINS: Self-styled investment counselors, entrepre-
neurs, confidence men.

PLOT: Victims are promised high profits from investing
their money for a short time in a scheme. The villain
makes a reputation to attract more investors by "doubling
the money" of his first customers, paying them off with
funds taken from later clients. After that he starts putting

more of the money into his pocket and giving less to his customers. Since he does not invest the money it does not "grow," and eventually the pyramid collapses.*

The acknowledged master of pyramiding was a clever little Bostonian, Charles Ponzi. He went into business in the 1920s as an "investment counselor." His only assets were a fast lip, an air of confidence and the ability to spellbind listeners with a get-rich-quick dream. Soon he was rolling through Boston's narrow streets in a cream-colored Cadillac limousine. One report tells that people shoved their money at him through the open windows when he stopped in traffic. That may not be true, but it is a fact that Ponzi was entrusted with more than $9 million by hopeful investors. He had a feel for public relations. Whenever a pretty girl or a member of one of the Back Bay aristocracy became a client he made certain that they received a quick return on their investment and that the press witnessed the payoff.

Although pyramiding is suicidal, it continues to hold a fascination for villains. And, as to why so many people have been so careless with their own money, there is apparently only one answer—the oldest one, greed.

An electronic-age version of the pyramid swindle recently came to light in Switzerland. The Florida man who was the brains behind this swindle made an almost scientific study of the pyramid method to extract money from a gullible public. From the experiences of others whose pyramids had collapsed he realized that collapse is inevitable. Their weakness, he concluded, was in not making sufficient preparations to protect themselves when the pyramid caved in on them—for one thing, they kept their victims' money close at hand, in a bank or vault, where it could be seized—and so he decided to

_____

*An exception is a middle-aged U.S. villain who is now serving a fifteen-year prison term. When caught he still had $6 million of the money given him by investors. He arranged for a bank to hold the money pending the outcome of suits by investors to recover it. Due to a technicality of the law they cannot sue until he finishes his prison term. Meanwhile the money is earning annual interest of $350,000, which the villain has ordered the bank to distribute to his victims. By the time he is released he can have discharged the debt by paying out the principal and interest and still be a millionaire in his own right.

place the proceeds beyond the reach of his victims. Another weakness he found was that most of the swindlers who use the pyramid method operate on their own, as "one-man shows." This was too vulnerable a position for him to be caught in—and so he decided to operate within the framework of a "legitimate" multinational organization. When the pyramid collapsed, prosecutions for fraud could not be started, under existing laws, unless and until the affairs of the companies were wound up. This could postpone prosecution for years.

The Florida man acquired a Swiss "shell company," Tiderift, in August 1970—according to a report from Britain's Department of Trade and Industry, submitted by Mr. Peter Millett, counsel for the Department, in High Court on June 15, 1972. He changed the name of the company to "Koscot Interplanetary" and opened a United Kingdom affiliate in Nottingham. A few months later he incorporated Koscot AG in Switzerland with a capital of 50,000 Swiss francs, and an address in Zurich.

British investigators who called at that address found that it had no staff, no organization, no furniture. It was merely a name on a letter box. But that is all that the villain needed. It was the pocket into which the money could be made to disappear.

The Koscot operation was concentrated in Great Britain, where it was represented as a marketing organization for cosmetics by the direct selling method. It would capitalize on the wide acceptance by housewives of "the Avon lady" and organizations who sell legitimately by the door-to-door and home party methods.

As it turned out, it is doubtful that the Florida man cared whether the firm sold a single lipstick or pot of face cream. He did invest a few thousand dollars in "demonstrator's kits," purchased from wholesale cosmetic manufacturers who specialize in putting up beauty aids under private labels for department stores, salons and shops, but he did not order stocks from which customers could be supplied.

His main concern was to establish a $25 million

pyramid—or rather a pyramid in which $25 million would rise to the top. Energies were devoted almost entirely to the structuring and organization of a hierarchy of persons through whom sales would supposedly be conducted—but who would in fact be the victims who fed money to the villain.

On the lowest level were the "beauty advisors," who would eventually be doing the actual selling. They were to be recruited by the supervisors, who would share in their commissions and also sell cosmetics themselves. The supervisors were in turn appointed by distributors, who were to receive an override on all commissions earned by their distributors and beauty advisors. The distributors reported directly to company management.

The Florida man hired sales managers who conducted meetings to recruit distributors and supervisors. These meetings were advertised in local newspapers: "Learn How to Become Your Own Boss—Nothing to Sell—Make More Money than You Ever Dreamed You Could Have! Come to Hotel XXX tomorrow evening at 7 o'clock. Free refreshments and gifts to all."

There were two or three speakers at these meetings. First there was the man who repeated advertised claims—be your own boss, nothing to sell, make money. He introduced the second speaker, who painted a glowing picture of the large profits to be derived from payments of money by supervisors or beauty advisors brought into the program. He explained that all the participant needed to do was to bring in five candidates to the next meeting.

The next speaker played the part of the marketing expert, an independent authority who belongs to many national organizations and who has friendly relations with politicians, government officials and perhaps even the police. He claimed that he had investigated the company and its program and that it "checked out perfectly."

After being lulled into a sense of security by this "expert," victims were ready for the next step. The first speaker again returned and showed the "demonstrator's kit." It contained more than $100 worth of cosmetics (his estimate), and—if victims signed up as distributor or supervisor—they could buy one for only $25 and receive as a "free gift" a beauty case to carry the salves and creams and rouges.

Then came the crunch. The second speaker appeared and explained that the company operated on a franchise basis. A distributor must pay a license fee of $3,500, giving him the right to appoint other distributors and supervisors. When each new distributor was appointed by him, he would receive $1,500. "All you need do is appoint three distributors and you begin to make money. From then on you're in the chips," the speaker said. A distributor could also appoint supervisors, who paid the company $1,500 for the license. For every supervisor he appointed directly, the distributor would receive $350, and for every supervisor appointed by one of his supervisors he would be paid $250 by the company, with $100 going to the sponsoring supervisor.

Using a chalkboard, the speaker showed how a typical distributor could make a clear profit of nearly $7,000 in the first months by just appointing relatives and friends as four distributors, seven supervisors and having those supervisors appoint eight more supervisors. "Everyone profits from every new member in his chain," the speaker said.

Beauty advisors were outside the licensing arrangement. Significantly, very little was said of them in the program—and there was no mention at all of training to sell cosmetics, taking orders, delivering goods and the like. The object, of course, was to make every person coming to one of these meetings see ahead of him endless payments for bringing in more people.

"We chose the name Koscot Interplanetary because you can make your distribution organization grow to astronomical size," the speaker said.

The final word, before the meeting closed and coffee was served, was: "Anyone who gets in on this opportunity in the next few weeks will make a fortune."

During coffee time the speakers circulated among the

candidates, advising them on how they could raise the money for a distributorship. "Sorry, you can't buy a distributorship on monthly payments. Perhaps your banker . . . "

Many people left these meetings with their heads filled with astronomical figures of the money they were going to make just by getting five people to come to the next meeting. Then the next week the newly recruited five would bring in five more each and each one would mean money. The next week the twenty-five would each bring in five—more money. By the third week they would have to begin thinking about booking the Royal Albert Hall to hold the crowd. If all went according to the speaker's plans, before the end of the twelfth week some 130 million people would be involved in the cosmetics sales program.

Of course, nothing like that ever happened. The meetings kept struggling to get the first five off the ground. Rarely more than two meetings were justified in any one town, but in the first fifteen months of operation Koscot Interplanetary (U.K.) dropped over $1 million into the Florida promoter's "pocket" in Zurich, paid an additional $200,000 to salesmen and in kickbacks to distributors, and covered start-up expenses.

The Florida man was making plans to open up in West Germany and Holland, with Sweden to follow, when Britain's Department of Trade and Industry obtained a court order closing down Koscot Interplanetary on the grounds that it was a "public swindle."

The Florida man was ready to meet this eventuality. His proceeds were safe, in a numbered Swiss bank account—and tax free, thanks to his foresight. British law forestalled prosecution for fraud until the company was wound up. That would take years. And even then he could not be touched in Florida by Scotland Yard for this kind of an offense.

In recent years more and more people have been attracted to the idea of starting up their own pyramid money machines. A substantial number of them have escaped prosecution because the cost of collecting sufficient evidence to build a case for conviction is too great, or because after months of investigating the prosecutors do not feel they have enough evidence to present in court.

The growth in incidence of this fraud is apparent, however, when we compare the numbers of cases that do reach the courts. In 1973 there were forty-two cases of pyramid selling in U.S. criminal courts, an increase of 40 percent over the average number of cases heard annually between 1955 and 1965. Great Britain's courts had no such cases for four years, then in 1973 it had three. In the same year there were four in France, two in Germany, two in Sweden and five in Italy. None of these countries had more than one pyramiding case in any previous year since 1955. The evidence presented at these trials revealed the interesting fact that well-known banks and business firms had supplied financing to villains to start up their pyramid operations—and were sometimes among the victims when the pyramid collapsed.

Among frauds perpetrated by individuals who are out and out blackmailers is one sometimes called "Irma La Douce." This particularly nasty game is worked almost every day in big cities throughout the world when conventions are in town.

THE "IRMA LA DOUCE" HUSTLE

VICTIMS: Convention participants looking for prostitutes.

VILLAINS: Blackmailers working as pimps, hustlers.

PLOT: Contact is made in the convention hotel, meeting hall, bar, on the street. The villain looks for a victim who is wearing a convention badge. He discovers that the victim would be interested in a girl. He praises the girls at a certain back-street hotel. They are not only good-looking and know their jobs, but all have regular health checkups.

"It's a clean place," the villain says. "We don't allow

any soldiers or sailors going up there. And you won't carry any diseases back home with you."

He makes a deal with the victim. The price is right. He tells the victim that if he wants to pay with a credit card or travellers' check it will be accepted. The villain collects the fee for the girl and gives in return a ticket or poker chip. If a credit card is used, the villain has the charge slips in his pocket, which he fills out and the victim signs.

On the way to the hotel, the villain talks about the various girls the victim can choose from. He may even show some photos of girls in lewd poses. At the hotel, the villain takes him upstairs to a room. Outside the door he says: "This is a clean place; you have to have a VD test before you can go upstairs."

He opens the door. The hotel room has been temporarily converted into a makeshift clinic in the charge of a sexy-looking girl dressed in a nurse's uniform.

If the victim has picked a girl from the photos, the villain says: "I'll have your girl ready for you when you have had your VD examination." Then he leaves the man with the nurse.

She directs him to lay on his back on a cot and proceeds to strip off his trousers and underwear to examine his penis. Then she pricks his finger, takes a drop of blood and puts it into a test tube with some clear liquid. Instantly the liquid changes color. (This is nothing like the accepted medical tests for venereal diseases.)

When the man has dressed himself, the nurse asks him to sign a card. "I don't get paid for the test unless I have a signed card," she explains.

Then, as soon as she has put the card in a locked drawer, she tells the victim: "Sorry, but the test was positive. You have VD. You should see a doctor for treatment."

The victim leaves the small hotel full of anxiety. He forgets about having a girl, and even the money he paid—usually no more than $10.

While the victim is worrying about having VD, the nurse is busy. She takes a negative from a hidden camera, processes it and then makes a print. This is a very special print in which she uses two negatives, one superimposed upon the other. The resulting picture shows the half-naked victim in a compromising pose with a nude girl, the nurse.

Later, the victim receives a visitor at the hotel—the nurse, still in uniform. She may call him on the house telephone. "I have some good news for you," she says. "Is there somewhere we can talk in private?" He probably invites her to his room.

"There was an error in the test," she tells the victim. "I made a mistake. You do not have VD."

While the victim is enjoying a sense of relief, she puts the bite onto him. Shouldn't he show his appreciation to her for making a special trip to relieve him of worry—say $500?

If he hesitates she shows him the photograph, the credit card slip with his signature or the travellers' check and the VD card which he signed. It was blank when he put his signature on it, but it now bears a printed rubber stamp statement: "I am a customer in a house of prostitution and I voluntarily submit to a VD test. Further, I agree to pay for damages to persons or property while on these premises."

The nurse tells him that photocopies of these documents will be mailed to his wife or to his employer unless he gives her $500. If he pays, he can keep the documents. Of course, this time only cash is accepted.

Only rarely do the victims go to the police. When this has happened and the nurse and pimp have been arrested, their lawyer can argue that they were only supplying an unlicensed health service—and he has got the documents to prove it.

A man and woman who operated this swindle in the south of France were collecting $1,500 to $2,000 a day.

As soon as the press and television began talking about the energy crisis and the need to conserve fuels, the villains in the United States, Canada, Great Britain, and other countries put the old, familiar furnace fraud into high gear. They hired and trained new salesmen and began block-by-block coverage in many cities and towns.

THE FURNACE FRAUD—1974 VERSION

The salesman rang the doorbell of the victim during the day and found the housewife home. He introduced himself as an agent of a furnace-cleaning company. He showed her newspaper clippings stressing the importance of conserving coal, oil and gas, and advised her that it was everybody's duty to make sure that their home heating plant was operating at peak efficiency. As a public service, he said, his company was cleaning and inspecting all of the furnaces in the neighborhood. He even showed her orders he had just taken from one or two neighbors on her own street.

"Our company has a truck in this area and we are offering a special price of $24.95 for cleaning and inspecting a heating plant," he claimed. "It barely covers our costs, but we feel we must do our part in the fuel crisis."

He showed her a list which spelled out what the cleaning job included: checking all thermostats and valves, letting air out of radiators in hot water and steam systems, cleaning all pipes, decarbonizing burners and pilot lights, cleaning combustion chamber, descaling heat exchange pipes, etc. The victim agreed to have the furnace cleaned and signed the contract.

About two days later, a maintenance truck arrived with a team of servicemen. Upon completion of cleaning the furnace, one of the servicemen asked to use the victim's telephone. Making certain that she could hear what he said, he telephoned his office and asked to speak to the "furnace technician." He told him that he thought the furnace needed inspection. It did not seem to be operating properly. He arranged with the housewife to be at home when the inspector came that afternoon. Since there was a note of urgency in his manner, she canceled her plans to go shopping and waited for the inspector.

A man arrived and made an examination of the heating plant. "You're lucky not to have been poisoned by the gases," he told her. "Your furnace is warped and the seams of the firebox are separating. You need a new furnace."

The housewife said he would have to speak to her husband about that. The inspector agreed to stop by that evening on his way home—"because your heating plant is really dangerous."

That evening he returned and explained to both husband and wife that their furnace was faulty and could give off fatal fumes at any time—fumes that normally go up the chimney. He drew sketches of a warped and split heat exchanger unit to illustrate his argument.

Before he left, the husband signed a written contract agreeing to purchase a new furnace on a time payment contract, which included installation and finance charges, for a total of $1,095.88.* They gave the required down payment of 10 percent.

The next day, the husband had second thoughts. He called the company from whom he had been buying fuel and asked them to send one of their engineers around to look at his heating plant. The inspection was made and the engineer found the furnace to be up to standard and in no way faulty.

On the basis of that information the husband immediately wrote a letter to the firm from whom he had ordered the new heating plant to cancel his order. He received a prompt reply, from the firm's lawyer. It explained that the contract he had signed was irrevocable and that among other things he had accepted the inspector's diagnosis as binding. Within an hour after the postman delivered the lawyer's letter, a crew arrived and ripped out the old heating plant and carted it away.

The family was without a furnace for nearly a week before the new one arrived and was installed.

The husband refused to pay the first installment payment, because he had cancelled the order. They had no right to do what they did, he insisted. But the con men had the law on their side. As he had defaulted on a

---

*The Better Business Bureau, who supplied me with details of these frauds, says the furnace in this case was a standard $610 model.

payment, under the terms of the contract he signed the company could demand the balance in full—which its lawyer did. The case wound up in the courts, where the husband was ordered to pay up—which he did.

Not until much later did this case come to the attention of the police, in the course of an investigation of the fraudulent furnace company. By then it was too late to give this victim much relief. They advised him to be more careful about what he signed in the future.

ALL THAT SMELLS AROUND THE OIL COMPANIES MAY NOT BE PETROLEUM

"The oil companies may find it difficult to convince the public that . . . they have not been involved in conspiracies, frauds and other forms of corruption," states an editorial in the *Wall Street Journal* of January 29, 1974.

In 1973 when the Middle East oil crisis cut supplies, the steep rise in international oil prices caused many oil companies to step up their pressure on the governments. These pressures included:

● making false reports about the state of supplies and reserves;

● influencing public officials and politicians to get them to approve price increases;

● threatening to move refineries and facilities to other countries if government concessions are not granted;

● operating with almost total autonomy in regard to distribution of oil stocks;

● making private deals with oil-producing countries contrary to the public interest.

Not all these pressures were applied in every country— and not every oil company applied pressures. There were some pressures applied that we still do not know anything about, and we may never know.

As this is being written, the oil fraud scandal in Italy has received the greatest public attention. Documents confiscated by an elite police Fraud Squad from Unione Petrolifera (Petroleum Industry Association) and various banks in Rome raise questions of false information relating to the oil supply situation and payoffs to government officials. Judicial proceedings for corruption and fraudulent price increases were started against Domenico Albonetti (president of Unione Petrolifera), Riccardo Garrone (chairman of the third largest Italian oil group), and others.

In Great Britain, the United States and other countries, government spokesmen, politicians and some sectors of the press charged that the oil companies made too much profit while consumers got too little fuel. It is true that at the same time that the oil men were trying to explain that a good share of their 1973 earnings were due to unusual factors—devaluation of dollars against other currencies held in large amounts by the companies, one-time accountability gains from foreign investments, etc.—their earnings reports showed record results.

For the first time in its history, Exxon's chairman called a press conference. "We are not making windfall profits," he stated. Yet at that time the ink was not yet dry on Exxon's 1973 report, which shows the highest earnings ever reported by an industrial company—$2,440,000,000, an increase of 59 percent over 1972. Gulf showed an even higher percentage increase, 60 percent.

Gulf's president, Z. D. Bonner, was one of several top oil company officials summoned to Washington by a Senate panel making an inquiry into the energy crisis in January 1974. "They made me feel like I was at a criminal trial," Bonner told the press afterward.

What was carefully avoided by the oil companies in giving testimony is the tax breaks they enjoy. For example, Mobil reported 1973 profits of $843 million, an increase of 47 percent over 1972. A substantial amount of this came from the fact that they were able to write off taxes paid to oil-supplying countries on their U.S. tax returns. Of the total price of oil paid by Mobil in Saudi Arabia—$7.12 a barrel—only ten cents represents actual production costs and $1.46 is the royalty payment. The balance—$5.56—is the tax paid to Saudi Arabia, which Mobil credited dollar for dollar against its U.S. income tax. Together, all U.S. oil companies wrote off over $3 billion in U.S. income taxes for 1973.

At the same time that the hearings in Washington were looking into the activities of the oil companies, other investigators gathered evidence that has led to the indictment of sixty people in the United Kingdom, Germany and the United States. They are alleged to have exploited the public concern over fuel reserves to persuade investors to put money into various fraudulent schemes. The accusations include misappropriation of funds from oil development projects, making false statements about drilling programs, selling unregistered securities and other forms of corruption.

Large fraud schemes, related to the drilling in the North Sea oil fields, are currently under investigation. According to an official directing one probe, some of the evidence already assembled might be damaging enough to shake several international oil companies to their very foundations.

9

Pirates: Thieves Who Steal Flicks, Patents and Computer Programs

As business has become international, so too have the pirates and bootleggers who steal for illegal profits. The fact that the problem has become commonplace is illustrated by the numerous legal battles over patents that protect inventions and copyrights that protect books, music and films going on around the globe.

As this is being written, Eastman Kodak Company and Polaroid Corporation are engaged in litigation over a patent on instant photography in Great Britain. General Electric Company has brought suit in Japan against a Japanese firm for allegedly infringing certain G.E. patents involving the marking of industrial diamonds. Major U.S. steel companies are being sued in American courts for allegedly infringing on a steelmaking invention—the oxygen process—claimed by some Austrians. An invention to aid offshore oil drilling was the subject of a court battle just settled in Great Britain between several big U.S. oil firms and British companies. An American phonograph-record maker is suing a Dutch company for making bootleg copies of its hit records and combining them in albums.

The widely varying rules and regulations governing

patents and copyrights in different nations make the job of protecting oneself against pirates and bootleggers increasingly complex. "The international patent scene is a real jungle," says Aram Kevorkian, a New York expert on international patent problems. François Panel, chief of the patent department at Compagnie Générale d'Electricité, a French electrical products manufacturer, adds: "If we are involved in litigation over one patent in various nations, we can't be sure of getting the same decision [from the courts]. We are only sure of getting different decisions."

Because of varying interpretations of laws, a pirate who was held guilty of infringing the rights of an American TV film company—he made 8mm copies of some of their films for sale to home-movie buyers—in West Germany and France was found innocent in Britain and Italy. These decisions upset a whole series of licensing agreements that the American company had laboriously worked out for distribution of home-movie versions of its films in European countries.

BOOTLEG MOVIE RACKET

While on a holiday at a resort hotel in Portugal in 1973, an official of a motion picture studio took his family to the lounge one evening when the hotel was screening a movie for its guests. The film was *The Day of the Jackal.* A week later, after his return to Hollywood, this producer was invited by a friend to a sneak-preview of a major studio feature—*The Day of the Jackal.*

"Sorry, I saw it last week in Portugal," he said, turning down the invitation.

"But that's impossible! The only prints are still here at the studio. We finished the editing just three weeks ago and ran the film for our distributors. It'll be in the vault until tomorrow's screening."

An investigation revealed that the messenger who picked up the print at the private screening room where it had been shown to distributors did not deliver it to the studio vault until the following morning. During the night it had been copied by a technician who used the equipment in a laboratory where he was employed. Many copies were made. The film stock used to make the negative and prints was stolen by the employee from the laboratory's supplies.

Within a day, the illegal prints of *The Day of the Jackal* were on their way to Europe, concealed under clothing in the luggage of a courier employed by a bootlegger. Bootleg prints are usually smuggled across national borders, since many countries have tight restrictions on the importation of films, which are usually delayed in clearance through customs.

It is estimated that several thousand people in Europe saw *The Day of the Jackal* before its world premiere. Detectives found that one of the prints had even been copied in a laboratory operated by nuns of a Catholic religious order just outside of Rome by a technician who services the duplicating and processing equipment. He is said to have sold four prints to film clubs and collectors for $1,000 each—at a profit to him of nearly $700.

Important feature films are highly desirable for the "bootleg" trade, but the bulk of the business is in old standards that people enjoy seeing again and in films that have not yet been shown on television. Among the more widely copied films are: *Billy the Kid* (*"The Left-handed Gun*, with Paul Newman"—retitled by the bootleggers); *The Boston Strangler; The Barefoot Contessa; A Star Is Born; Doctor Zhivago; The Bridge on the River Kwai; Anatomy of a Murder; Bus Stop;* and films starring Humphrey Bogart, Laurel and Hardy, Judy Garland, Marilyn Monroe, Jack Palance, and Brian Donlevy, as well as films directed by Alfred Hitchcock, John Ford, Josef von Sternberg—among others.

The almost new condition of two feature films he bought as "junk" for about $400 aroused the suspicions of British comedian Bob Monkhouse, who has a library of nearly 500 films collected since World War II. He could not understand why they had been junked; they were far from being ready for the scrap pile. In search of the answer to the riddle, Monkhouse put detectives onto a "piracy" swindle that led to what is perhaps the first prosecution for conspiracy to defraud film companies by unlawfully copying and distributing films and breaking copyright. The case was tried in the Old Bailey in October 1973.

In May 1972, Monkhouse bought the two nearly perfect films and started asking questions. The movements of cans of film to and from London theaters were placed under surveillance by Scotland Yard. It was found that two feature films had "disappeared" from the New Victoria Cinema, London. The chief projectionist at the Cinema, Cyril Whiting, told detectives that he had "borrowed" several films during the previous years and had passed them on to a friend who made copies. He did not consider it was wrong to do this.

"Everybody does it," Whiting said in his sworn statement. "I even know of cases where stars of films buy copies made in this way because the studios won't give them prints. Nobody has ever complained."

(Further inquiries revealed that the film copy racket is on an international scale and that film producers have been defrauded of as much as $200 million annually in revenues from theatrical and TV showings. Stolen or "borrowed" films belonging to major studios were copied and distributed. Many of them turned up in resort hotels for the entertainment of guests, on nonscheduled airlines for showing to passengers, and even in the collections of Arab leaders, some of whom are believed to possess libraries of 3,000 to 5,000 films—many of them illegal prints. Customs men inspecting a hijacked airliner discovered a cargo of forty-seven recent films, some not yet released, en route to a film library in Israel. Every one was an illegal copy. It is believed that they were destined for the Arab market.)

Ten men were put on trial as the result of the first phase of the investigation. They include a former Paramount

Pictures projectionist, twenty-five-year-old John Avery, and the retired owner of Midland Film Library, seventy-two-year old Arthur H. Turner. Turner admitted in court to conspiring to steal films from Technicolor, Ltd., and to receiving the stolen print of a film. He was given twelve months in prison, suspended, a $1,400 fine and $2,250 costs. Avery and Whiting received prison terms of twelve and eighteen months respectively.

Detectives and victimized film producers were critical of the light punishments imposed. "A chauffeur who steals his employer's auto for a weekend can expect a stiffer penalty upon conviction," a Scotland Yard officer told me. "Yet the losses these men caused were enough to buy a fleet of Rolls-Royces."

What is probably the highest-priced film in the "pirate" market is one that was never made to be shown in theaters or on television. It is a private production by editors from several major Hollywood studios. Titled *Clips from the Cutting-Room Floor,* it is made up entirely of lengths of film which were edited out of feature films. It includes scenes in which gusts of wind have accidentally blown actresses' skirts over their heads; scenes in which costumes have fallen leaving actresses and actors standing nude and very embarrassed. One clip of a bedroom love scene played by two world famous stars was made by a second camera while the principal camera was focused on head and shoulders closeups of the scene. It shows the pair, surrounded by the film crew and equipment, are really "going all the way." Another scene shows Fred Astaire slipping and falling off the top of a grand piano while doing a tap dance routine; there is a bewildered John Wayne attempting a fast draw with a gun that is stuck in the holster; there is Vincent Price breaking out in laughter while playing a monster when the pretty virgin he has just slaughtered sneezes and dabs her nose with a Kleenex; and there are many dialogue fluffs or bloopers. An actor pulling back from a tender embrace with Marilyn Monroe remarks: "My God, you've got smelly armpits!" The line was not in the script.

A print of *Clips,* if you can find one, will cost at least $7,500—which tops by several thousand dollars the prices being asked for prints of *Deep Throat,* featuring sex athlete Linda Lovelace, or the uncut version of the film *Venus in Sables,* a study of perversion.

STEALING COMPUTER PROGRAMS

The sets of instructions that tell computers how to process data, when to add amounts, when to subtract, when to choose between two amounts, when to store information in a memory are known to be worth a fortune. These computer "programs" take months and even years to prepare by specially trained programmers and analysts. The investment in labor costs and computer time for experimental runs of new programs usually runs into the tens of thousands of dollars. Some programs have cost over half a million dollars to develop before they were ready to process one item of data. But once a program is produced it is like ready-to-wear clothing. It will fit the needs of many people. Programs direct computers to perform specific functions. One program tells a computer how to process all of the paperwork to put out an employee payroll—even to printing the paychecks. Another program directs a computer that supervises the machines used to bottle beer—from washing out the empty bottles all through the various steps until the freshly filled and capped bottles are automatically put into shipping cases and set off to a warehouse. Still other programs tell computers how to analyze information for business managers, how to forecast the number of boxes of cornflakes that *each* of 2,800 supermarkets will need six weeks from today to meet customer demands (based on needs in previous years and taking into account changes in tastes, population shifts, changes in the cost of living and other pertinent factors), and so on.

There are also programs that instruct computers in highly sophisticated operations which assist scientists, technicians, navigators, educators, engineers and others in their work.

Since a cornflakes marketing program developed, let us say, by Kellogg at great expense can be used with some modification by any of the companies around the world who produce and sell cornflakes, there is a market for copies of these programs. Perhaps Kellogg doesn't sell copies of its market forecast program—they probably want to keep it secret to give them a competitive advantage. But if a "pirate" made copies of the Kellogg program he would have no difficulty in selling it to competitors at a high price. He could command any price that is lower than what it would cost a buyer to develop a similar program for himself.

Of course, many computer users do trade programs with other computer users. There are also suppliers of prepackaged programs, called "software houses," who offer standard programs to perform widely used functions such as payroll, inventory control, traffic-light sequencing and the like. Some of these software houses started in business because the people who promoted them pirated programs from commercial firms. The copies of programs they sell thus cost them nothing beyond the price of the reels of magnetic tape on which they are printed.

Not long ago the Swiss subsidiary of a multinational U.S.-based chemical company ordered some packaged programs from a software house in France. When the programs arrived the Swiss data-processing people discovered that they had bought programs which were exact copies of those developed by their parent company in the United States. The French software pirates had not even bothered to change the values to the metric system.

Highly confidential proprietary computer programs are carefully guarded by their owners: an airline reservation system program, or one for analyzing trends in stock market prices, or a program to run an automated factory. If a pirate can get his hands on one of these he could retire for life.

SPY-PROOF SECURITY—IS IT POSSIBLE?

Technicians working in the physical security devices field must get ulcers from frustration. Every time they come up with a new piece of sophisticated equipment to prevent intruders and industrial espionage agents from gaining access to company property, the intruders and spies find ways to defeat them.

Recently, several companies brought out electronic push-button locks—a sophistication on the manual combination lock concept. For a time they made things difficult for intruders. But after a few months users began to complain that unauthorized persons were getting by these locks. How?

In return for not being prosecuted an industrial spy, captured in the corporate offices of a Manchester, England, firm by security guards, offered to explain to them how he did it. He led them to the door and pointed to the lock. It had ten numbered push buttons.

"See those four dirty buttons, greasy with fingermarks?" he said. "They are the ones that are being used. The other six are practically clean. This reduced tremendously the number of buttons I had to push to figure out the combination and open the door."

For centuries passwords have been used to separate intruders from those who belong. This method is the least expensive—and probably worth the least. Passwords are often given away by people to anybody else who is working with them on the job. A temporary secretary at St. Regis Paper Company in New York was given the password and code numbers needed to gain access to the company's computer systems. She jotted them down in her dictation notebook, which she carried to her next job. It happened to be a competitor, and she gave one of their executives the password and codes. He happened to be honest, and he telephoned St. Regis and told them they ought to change their password at once.

Passwords are a problem, but they are inexpensive. Several corporations have invented schemes to strengthen passwords. One firm gives out a new password at the end of every transaction. This is not very effective because once an unauthorized person learns the password he can use it, while the authorized user is locked out.

Another scheme, called "hand-shaking," requires the inquirer seeking information from the computer to correctly answer a personal question, something known only to him, before he can find out what he wants to know. This slows down the running of a business. I remember sitting in the office of a man who has a computer terminal on his desk. In the middle of our conversation a question came up and he said: "Wait a minute. I'll get the answer from our computer." He put the question in by typing on the keyboard. The terminal's screen lit up and displayed another question: "In what month was your mother-in-law born?"

He growled with irritation as he punched out the answer: "March." The words "Thank you. That's correct," flashed on the screen.

"This damn machine is fighting with me all day while I'm trying to get my job done." he said, as we waited for the reply to his original question.

Some access control devices are so dramatic that one suspects they were designed for science-fiction films rather than for practical use. For instance, there is a handprint reader that squirts a purple dye on the hand of any unauthorized person who tries to use it to open a door. One wonders why they did not go all the way and put in a guillotine to cut off the fingers.

A guillotine might also be a good attachment for another personnel verification device patented recently by a Canadian professor. Working on the theory that everybody's head has a distinctive shape, he developed a piece of equipment that reads the bumps on the heads of all persons who are authorized to enter through a locked gate. This information is digitized and stored in a computer. To open the lock, you step up to a box with a large hole and stick your head into it. Little feelers come down and take measurements which are relayed to the computer. If these measurements compare favorably with a set already in the computer's memory, the gate automatically unlocks. If not—well, why not the guillotine?

The Japanese have been working on a lip print reader. They argue that lip prints are as unique as fingerprints and easier to read. I thought about coming in to work and kissing the Xerox machine to get it started. The Japanese do such wonderful things with plastics that perhaps they will install their lip reader in a life-size dummy of Elizabeth Taylor for males (and maybe one like Robert Redford for the females) to be set up outside the doors to sensitive areas.

The entertainment value of these notions is unquestionably high, while their practical value is just as unquestionably close to zero.

Already in wide use are the identity cards with magnetic stripes laminated inside. When inserted into a reader, they identify the holder by information previously magnetically recorded. If it is the correct information he gains access, if not an alarm is given. However, the magnetic stripes can be accidentally erased. I know one man who lost his identity by driving his car through a radar-monitored speed trap.

COMPUTER SOFTWARE PIRATES

In 1972 the operator of a Paris software house raided more than one hundred U.S. industrial, public utility and banking and retail computer centers and succeeded in stealing most of their confidential programs.

The operator posed as a professor of Computer Science at a well-known French university. The operator was ingenious enough to offer to teach a course that would orient students to the use of computers without any cost to the university. Since the university was not then offering such a course and could not afford to hire someone to teach it, they accepted his offer for a fall series of thirteen lectures. This man met his class six times, and then failed to show up for the remaining classes. During those first six weeks he had obtained a supply of the university's official letterheads on which he wrote airmail letters to more than 200 computer centers in the United States. In each he stated that he was coming to America in search of knowledge of programming and software technology, which was much further advanced than in France. The information he obtained was to be used for teaching purposes only. Would the computer centers receive him and help him while he was in the United States? More than one hundred replied that they would welcome his visit. The replies were addressed to him in care of the French university. This made it all seem quite legitimate. Not one of the American firms took the trouble to check further on him.

As soon as he had received over a hundred replies he bought his ticket to New York. For seven months he toured the United States visiting the computer centers. He made such a convincing impression on some of the industrial companies he visited that they picked up his hotel expenses. One Michigan chemicals company put him up at their country club. Everyone was very cooperative and went to a great deal of effort to supply almost everything he asked for—including copies of some programs that normally were kept under lock and key. A Maryland firm gave him free run of their computer center during a weekend and permission to copy any of their program tapes that he might require. They even refused to let him pay for the reels of tape on which he made copies.

When this man was ready to return to France he had so many program tapes that he could not afford to fly and take them as baggage, so he took a freighter out of Boston.

Back in Paris he leased computer tape copying machines and photocopy equipment. He installed these in an unused bedroom of his home. Then he started a software mail-order house, sending brochures to computer users throughout Europe. In the first week he received more than two dozen orders for his "off-the-shelf" programs. The income covered all of his expenses for the trip to America and setting up his business. At the end of the first six months he had netted over $80,000 and was employing a staff of nine.

The whole story of his piracy scheme might never have come to light if a Minneapolis flour milling company had not discovered that he was selling copies of one of their top-secret computer programs. It was not one they had given to him, but a program that he had bribed a company employee to copy. (He had offered to send the man a case of champagne from France; it never arrived.) The Minneapolis firm lodged a complaint against him with French police, who raided his headquarters and seized all of the tapes. He pleaded guilty to the charge of dealing in stolen property and paid a fine of about 5,000 francs. After that all of his program tapes were returned to him, except the one he obtained in Minneapolis.

Late in 1973 this enterprising pirate moved his operations to Italy and began exporting programs to Japan, Australia, the Middle East, the Eastern bloc countries and Red China, as well as to Western Europe. A few days before this was written I received a notice in the mail that he has just opened a branch in Argentina.

10

Security
Is Your Business

On September 5, 1972, the day after a busy Labor Day weekend at New York airports, a theft of $45,000 from an airline office in midtown Manhattan was reported to the police. A month later, on October 10, (after Columbus Day weekend) the same ticket bureau was robbed of $33,000. Again, on November 27, following the Thanksgiving Day holiday weekend, the ticket office was hit for a third time, with a loss of $48,000. In each incident, the same manager and his entire staff were ambushed as they opened the office in the morning by four men wearing stockings over their heads and carrying weapons. Each time, all employees were tied up until the gang opened the safe and took the money. The first time they forced the manager at gunpoint to give them the safe's combination numbers. The second and third time this was unnecessary: The combination had not been changed.

These robberies were not only very carefully planned in detail, but the villains had a full knowledge of the layout of the building and its access points. They entered the ticket bureau through a trap-door skylight in the manager's office and dropped onto his desk—there were footmarks found on his desk blotter. At 8:20 A.M., when the staff of four entered the bureau through a side door, they found themselves face to face with shotguns.

Before carrying away their loot, one of the villains handed the manager a note—at each of the three roberies—which claimed that the raids had been carried out to raise funds for a Middle Eastern terrorist group. Police did not take the claims very seriously. They believe that it was a Mafia criminal raid, camouflaged by political allegations. But the possibility that the claims are true cannot be disregarded. Political extremists frequently obtain their funds by raids on businesses, banks and cash in transit.

The success of these robberies was due almost entirely to the fact that the villains could operate unobserved behind the closed door of the manager's office—where the safe was also located. The fact that the staff used the rear entrance is an obvious security weakness. It provided ideal ambush conditions for the villains.

After the first raid, it is impossible to explain why security precautions were neglected. Within one block of the ticket bureau there are three banks, all with night depositories. Why wasn't the money put into one of them?

The ambush technique is so common in banks and other places that handle large amounts of cash that defensive procedures have been developed and workers trained in their use. No one suggests that employees should argue with villains with guns in their hands, but there are other ways to deal with ambush situations.

Some firms have already put into operation training which enables employees to avoid walking into an ambush. But at the New York ticket bureau the staff obviously had had no training. If they had entered one by one, a few minutes apart, it would have given those still outside the bureau an opportunity to call police when the ambushers made their first move. They should also have entered using both the front and rear doors, with an employee who has entered at the back being required to pass through the ticket counter section of the bureau—in full view of the public street—to admit another employee. And why was there no peephole or burglar chain on the rear door which the staff could have used before admitting someone through it?

These villains must have been delighted to find everything in their favor three times within as many months. It is astonishing that the only people who seem to learn from experience are the villains. Each of the security loopholes in this case is exactly the kind which villains seek out and exploit—and they repeat it over and again.

In this age of electronic data processing it should not be too difficult a task for the details of "repeat" crimes to be carefully collated and assessed to provide a basis for a systematic analysis of all likely techniques of criminal attacks on various types of businesses—banks, jewelry shops, supermarkets, etc. With such information in hand businessmen would be able to plan better physical security—without costly excessive designing—and to train their employees to anticipate visits from villains and be prepared to cope with them.

SECURITY CATCHPHRASES

People constantly parrot security catchphrases that in the end are responsible only for lulling them into a false sense of security. In spite of the many pieces of catchphrase security advice, it is impossible, for example, to convey the impression that a house or shop or office is occupied when it is not. One friend of mine followed all the rules before he took off with his family for three weeks in Spain. He found them on a checklist that came in the mail:

STOP THE NEWSPAPERS AND MILK AND THE MAIL.

CLOSE AND LOCK ALL YOUR WINDOWS.

INSTALL A TIME SWITCH SO THAT YOUR LIGHTS WILL COME ON AFTER DARK AND GIVE THE IMPRESSION YOU ARE AT HOME.

BUT DO NOT LEAVE A LIGHT ON IN THE

ENTRY HALL; IT WILL TELL EVERYONE YOU
ARE OUT.

And so on. Upon his return, he found that his home had
been burglarized in spite of all these precautions. He
called the local police crime prevention officer and demanded to know how the villains discovered that the
house was empty.

"Easy," said the crime prevention expert. "The grass
on your front lawn is two feet high!"

But there are other ways the villains could have found
out because he *did* follow the advice of the catchphrases.
If you are going to stop the newspapers, the milk delivery
and the mail you must tell the persons concerned. The
paper boy will know you are going away, so will the
milkman, and a little notice will be displayed on the
sorting bins at the post office for any employee to read.
If you notify the police and ask them to keep an eye on
your house, everybody at the local police station will
know.

Windows tightly closed on a hot summer day—with no
evidence of air conditioning—doesn't really prove that
you are at home.

When the time switch turns on the lights in the
evening, villains can see into your windows and determine that the house is unoccupied. If you close the
curtains, an unanswered knock at the door or an unanswered telephone call will reassure the villains that you
are only trying to fool them.

One man who does use a time switch in his shop leaves
his window shades up. If an intruder pulls any one of
them down while he breaks into the safe, the police are
likely to arrive very soon. On the outside of each window
shade the shop owner has painted in large letters: "CALL
THE POLICE. THIS SHOP IS BEING ROBBED."

As to the light in the entry hall being left off, this
homily, too, is misleading. A light left on in the hall
could easily mean that you are returning home soon.

In place of these hackneyed phrases, the piece of
advice which should be kept in mind is this one: *Try not*

to advertise your absence too much. Keep in mind that some of the conventional ideas about not advertising your absence may have an opposite effect.

People who carry payrolls and large amounts of cash are often told, "Always go at different times and choose different routes," the idea being that villains will find it more difficult to attack if you do not follow a fixed routine. The basic problem is that there are only so many ways you can travel through city streets between a bank and a place of business—and if oneway streets are involved the limitations on choice are even greater. Furthermore, a payroll must be delivered at the same time, on the same date, every payday, or else the employees will not be happy. This means that it must be transferred from the bank to the paymaster within certain time periods. For these practical reasons, villains can plan their hits within certain variables.

One firm has experienced the theft of several payrolls before it instructed its employees to go to the bank to receive their pay envelopes—or, rather, it had the bank come to their employees. On every payday an armored bank office trailer is driven into the factory and employees line up to receive their money.

The thing to remember about widely broadcast security catchphrases is that the villains hear of them too and make their plans accordingly. Such a catchphrase can easily become an open invitation to crime. The pretense of security is sometimes worse than no security at all.

When hardware stores in California began selling signs which read, "THESE PREMISES ARE PROTECTED BY THE GIBRALTAR ALARM SYSTEM," they sold hundreds to people who put them up to scare away burglars. Of course, they had no alarms. Villains started looking for these signs as indicating easy marks. Within three weeks there were 170 break-ins in the Greater San Francisco area, all at homes, shops and businesses displaying the Gibraltar Alarm signs.

Long-established practices, like long-echoed maxims, also tend to breed a false sense of security which is absolutely no defense against the determined villain.

RESPONSIBILITY TO ASK QUESTIONS

A computer operator, posing as a handyman, appeared every day for two weeks in the data-processing center of a major insurance company. He replaced a cracked glass in a partition, touched up scratched paint surfaces, remounted fluorescent ceiling lights, and among other chores gave the ladies' rest room a fresh wallcovering of paper in a delightful floral pattern. Everybody saw him doing these jobs. But what they did not see him doing was giving commands to the computer to issue checks to his order amounting to a total of $56,000. That did not come to light until three months after he had gone.

Who had hired him to do the odd jobs? No one knew. Why hadn't he been challenged, asked about the authorization for the work he did? No one knew. How could a stranger intrude on the computer center for ten consecutive work days and arouse no suspicion? Because everybody on the staff thought he was the responsibility of some other staff member.

It often appears that fraud is possible because no one individual considers it to be his responsibility to ask questions about people or proposals involved in everyday business. This means that many businessmen and supervisors limit their interest to matters within their own area of responsibility and fail to question the bona fides, integrity or viability of activities in other areas even when such activities raise suspicions in their minds. Perhaps they fear stepping on someone else's toes—but that is no excuse.

The vice-president of the French affiliate of a prominent international banking firm happened to see a newly hired assistant manager at a locksmith's waiting to have several duplicate keys made. He thought it odd and mentioned the incident to his secretary. She urged him to make an inquiry, but he was reluctant to do so. However, she did jot down a note on the subject in her diary. Four months later, when the assistant manager did not appear for work one morning and was found to have left the country, the discovery was made that over three dozen safe deposit boxes in the bank's vault has been unlocked and their contents stolen—uncut diamonds, negotiable stocks, cash, gold bars, an unpublished manuscript by a celebrated nineteenth-century author and a small collection of rare and valuable postage stamps.

The vice-president was stunned—but not by the breach of trust or by his own failure to act on his suspicions. What bothered him was the fact that his secretary told insurance company investigators and police about his report of seeing the assistant manager at the locksmith's. He was asked embarrassing questions and did not come off too well with his answers. He expressed less concern over the bank's loss than for his own loss of face. Within a few days he found an excuse to dismiss his secretary. Not long thereafter, his boss from New York paid him a visit and suggested that he apply for early retirement. He did.

In these days of managerial diversification, specialized responsibilities and multiple directorships it is perhaps understandable that many businessmen avoid responsibility outside their own limited areas. There is no reason why this need be tolerated, however. One remedy adopted by several dozen well-known American corporations is to appoint a very senior executive with a special responsibility for making delicate inquiries anywhere in the organization. Usually he reports only to the board of directors. In many companies his assignments include a systematic review of every aspect of company operations and personnel and to consider the risks of potential villainy attached to each.

In establishing such a post, management usually assumes that the majority of workers in the organization are honest and loyal and it is only seeking to reduce the risks of important losses. Most often these are fraud and theft.

RISK MANAGEMENT

Risk management is basically a simple concept. It is essentially commonsense judgment. We all practice it every day when making certain kinds of decisions:

"Shall I try to beat the red light at the next intersection?"

"Shall I take out travel insurance on the family for our holiday?"

"Shall I lay in a stock of foods on sale today to avoid paying higher prices later?"

These are very simple examples of risk management. Others often involve more complex analysis. But all are a matter of commonsense.

Risk management is "a continuous plan to (1) avoid events and circumstances that cause loss, and/or (2) lessen the operational financial effect of unavoidable loss at the lowest practicable cost," according to a leading American authority in the field, Edward W. Siver. It is a process involving loss prevention and loss funding. In order to manage a risk, according to Mr. Siver, it is necessary to review the operation that is to be protected. Order and method are essential here. The review covers three fundamental factors:

FACTOR	EXAMPLE
Identification of risk	If I take my girlfriend to a nightclub, my wife may find out about it.
Measurement of risk	If she does, she may leave me and file for divorce.
Handling of risk	Therefore I can say to my girl friend, "Put on your dancing shoes and we'll paint the town"—or "We'd better split a bottle at your apartment, darling, and listen to records."

One risk that many companies recognize is the possibility that the method used by a clever con man to commit a crime will become public knowledge and others will copy it. If they do, the company or other firms may suffer additional losses, and therefore they take steps to keep the method secret—even at the risk of compounding a felony. Computer users have done this, as have banks, investment houses, retail stores and airlines, among other businesses.

Steven Verzi, a fifteen-year-old California schoolboy, was accused by a teacher of trying to sneak into a basketball game without paying. The next time he was heard from he had stowed away on a Pan American nonstop flight to London. This was in February, 1974.

Steven spent a week with relatives in England, and then returned home on a ticket paid for by his father. But by then he had earned enough money to pay for the trip from selling exclusive rights to the story of his adventure to British newspapers and for a television appearance. One thing he did not reveal, however, is how he stowed away.

The airline's risk managers had decided on a policy regarding the incident. Steven Verzi's offense carries a stiff penalty upon conviction, and the evidence against him was enough to establish a *prima facie* case. But prosecution would entail public disclosure of his method, as would a full story in the press. Not surprisingly the airline did not want the method to be revealed, for it might supply the very information some political terrorist could use to plant a bomb on an airliner or to sneak aboard with an arsenal for a hijack attempt.

The option Pan American elected to use was described by Steven Verzi himself in a statement to a United Press reporter: "I have an agreement with Pan American," he says. "They won't charge me for the ticketless flight if I won't reveal how I got away with it."

Risks are not limited to large corporations. In fact, the small retail store owner or a householder is likely to be running a greater liability risk than a chain of stores. Many of the most cunningly devised and skillfully executed frauds and thefts are aimed at the small businessman and homeowner. Villains themselves often consider their risks too great in trying to "score" against a big business organization.

METHODS VILLAINS MAY USE

A risk reviewer studies the methods a villain is likely to use for committing crimes that include the prevention of their discovery and avoiding detection. Among the actual means by which business crimes may be carried out are the following:

THREAT—This category includes situations where the villain has taken possession of company property and refuses to return it on demand. For example, the man who is leaving to take a job with another company and who takes with him documents which are the proprietary information of his former employer with the intent to use the information to benefit his new employer. Also included are cases involving blackmail, extortion, and even threats of violence (sabotage, bombing, personal injury).

PROPERTY DAMAGE—Substantial damage to the property of the company, sometimes preceded by a threat. This damage can be both physical destruction and attacks on the firm's good name and reputation by "character assassination."

STEALTH—Many wrongdoings fall into this category. It includes cases in which the stolen items are not missed for a long time, until an audit or inventory perhaps; cases in which the crime is concealed in manipulations of computer data and functions, as in the generating of false records to cover thefts, or duplicating tapes; and cases in which an insider takes advantage of his access to the items to appropriate them.

DECEPTION—Cases in which villains commit frauds against the company, or use the company to defraud others—for example, the copying of a company trade mark on the packaging of an inferior product to fool the public.

CONFUSION—Creating confusion is a means employed by some villains to cover their crimes. The cover-up techniques can be employed either before the act or later to distract attention from the loss. In one case a villain spread a false rumor that a former employee had sold company secrets to a competitor, and then proceeded to sell the secrets himself. In another case, a company car used to carry the payroll to several outlying facilities developed an engine fire, exploded and burned to a cinder. Canvas sacks containing pay envelopes were totally destroyed. Scientific investigators studied the ashes and brought in evidence used to convict the payroll messenger. He had removed the money before setting fire to the vehicle.

ABUSE OF TRUST—This category includes both company employees and employees of outside organizations with whom trust relationships are maintained: consultants, lawyers, banks, etc. There are a number of reasons why these people may abuse their trust: Laziness or carelessness; yielding to extortion, blackmail; hostility or disloyalty to the company or particular staff members (conflict of personality) or loyalty to outside villains—family members, social contacts or members of some political, racial or national group. Any person who is a principal villain in a wrongdoing causing loss is implicitly an abuser of trust.

Crimes in business may involve a single short act, usually committed when the villain has both the opportunity and the temptation. Example: A night office cleaner discovers an unlocked cash box atop a file cabinet and steals the money. Or the crime may be a single act repeated over a substantial period. Example: A trusted bank employee milks funds from accounts for several months or years. Or the same villain may commit a series of crimes, employing a different means in each one. Example: A blackmailer who has the opportunity to steal (common theft) and to embezzle at various times.

ATTITUDES OF THE VILLAIN

No review of risks of fraud and theft is complete without considering the possible effects on him of the risks of discovery and punishment. A villain may regard the prospects of the discovery of the crime and of himself as the criminal in several ways. (1) He does not greatly care if the crime is discovered (a) even if the attempt has been unsuccessful or (b) so long as it is successful. He does want the crime to remain undiscovered if he plans to repeat it or so he can flatter himself with having perpetrated a "perfect crime." (2) He does not greatly care if he is identified (a) if he thinks himself immune from or insensitive to punishment, or (b) if he can place himself beyond the reach of punishment (as by fleeing to a foreign country from which he cannot be extradited).

Fear of punishment and the wish to avoid it are not compelling deterrents for many con men and thieves. Interviews with about sixty employees of a leading American bank, all of whom were caught in frauds or thefts over a period of two years, reveal that only 19 percent admitted giving any thought to the consequences of their crimes while committing them.

EFFECTS OF SECURITY PRECAUTIONS

The possible effects of various security precautions on the risk of fraud and theft are not easy to assess, because the element of chance plays a big role and security measures themselves are often vulnerable. However certain factors can be reviewed:

— The crime may not be attempted owing to the difficulty or cost of execution. Example: If parts of a piece of information are distributed among several persons or in different places, it is more difficult to get access to than if it is all in one place. Many firms are splitting up data related to important company secrets among several minicomputers instead of depositing all of it in one computer storage unit.

— If it is extremely unlikely that the crime cannot be committed without being detected, the villain may pass it by.

— Security precautions which make possible immediate discovery as soon as the crime is committed and increase the risk to the villain of being caught before he can get away may discourage him from making the attempt.

— If the crime may be discovered by routine security checks or audits at a later date, the villain who proposes to repeat his crime in the same place may abandon the scheme. Example: an official who embezzles small amounts regularly from his employer because he knows that a single large amount would be instantly detected will find it difficult to continue for a long time because of regular audits of accounts by auditors.

— Suspicion may be aroused leading to an investigation of a crime because the villain is in a place where he ought not be or because he is doing something extraordinary or because the commission of the crime would involve leaving suspicious evidence—any of these may deter a villain from the attempt. Examples: If a villain who works in the manufacturing plant would have to enter the cashier's office to steal the money he wants, he might think twice before doing it.

PROTECTION OF THE LAW

A proper evaluation of risks and options should include a review of the strengths and weaknesses of the protection the law affords against various kinds of fraud and theft. It would take several volumes to cover the various forms of protection that the laws in different countries provide against wrongdoing in business. In many cases it is found that there are no laws to cover certain kinds of situations—industrial espionage, wiretapping, illegal surveillance, etc. In other countries the laws on such violations are very clearly written and the penalties are stiff.

In growing numbers of cases in the courts these days the physical objects taken are of nominal value (power from a telephone line to make a wiretap recording, or a few sheets of computer print-out paper, or photocopy paper on which a document has been copied). But the value of the information contained in these documents may be worth millions. In imposing a penalty for theft of such items, courts must be guided by local laws. In some countries the court is entitled to take into account the harm done and the loss sustained by the taking of the information. But in other countries the laws do not grant courts such freedom. A villain who was convicted of stealing two sheets of photocopy paper containing a formula worth $12 million in development costs (which he sold to a competitor) received the maximum penalty —$25 and court costs. In another jurisdiction he could have been fined up to $50,000 and sent to prison for a maximum of fourteen years for the same offense.

More serious problems in gaining protection arise when the item taken is disembodied information, such as trade secrets carried away by the villain in his brain after being memorized. Is such an act theft? When an employee changes jobs he carries with him in his head certain proprietary information. He has appropriated that information but he does not deprive his former employer of its use. He simply deprives him of the benefits of exclusive possession. In terms of competitive advantages this may be a tremendous loss to the owner. Few courts will regard such acts as more than breach of trust; even then it is difficult to bring them within the terms of the law.

One of the most likely ways of losing proprietary information is through an employee who may inadvertently or deliberately transmit the information to someone who can profit from it. This is compounded in consultant services and computer bureaus where employees are bound by contract to keep client information confidential. If one of these employees talks too much the employer may also become liable for breach of contract.

Although it may not be adequate, about the only protection against such risks is the obvious one of choosing employees with care. Some restraints can also be applied by inserting conditions in the employment contract forbidding the communication of proprietary information to unauthorized persons during or after the period of employment without due authority. Other terms may restrict public speeches and writing for publication without prior approval, as these are frequent sources of leaks.

COMPUTER-ASSISTED FRAUD

Existing laws related to fraud have been extended in many countries to cover fraud by computer. Obtaining property by false pretenses or deception is descriptive of many offenses which can be carried out using a computer. Example: the case of a programmer who alters a computer program to cause deposits to be credited to his bank account with the intention of keeping the money. However, in cases where the villain does not obtain money but causes the computer to fail to report default on payment of his loan or to upgrade his credit rating, or similar actions not involving the direct loss of cash to the bank, prosecution may be difficult unless local laws include the offense of obtaining pecuniary advantage by deception.

Among the new laws which have been specifically written to cover fraud by computer, the most common are those referring to offenses in which a person who has access to a computer deliberately or with dishonest intent falsifies records stored in a computer in order to defraud the legitimate owners or users of the records. The types of offenses which prompted the enactment of these laws include: altering personnel records to delete unfavorable facts about an individual's history or to add false facts to improve the background; altering credit ratings; adding stocks to portfolios used as the basis for granting credit in order to deceive lenders; adjusting profit and loss figures for a company to gain more favorable tax advantages. The fact that most people regard computer records as completely true—"computers cannot lie"—makes the injury caused by false records all the more heinous.

In the eyes of the law, however, not all false records

can be labeled as forgeries. Forgery can be defined as the making of a false document in order that it may be used as genuine. But, in many countries, for a document to be labeled as a forgery in law courts it must not only lie but must lie about itself in such a way that it may be passed as genuine. It is the falsity in the purport of the document, not its contents, that constitutes forgery. This fine point handicaps the prosecution for forgery of a villain who falsifies a computer record, because the laws in most places do not yet identify a magnetic tape, disk or core as a "document."

INTRUSION, VANDALISM, SABOTAGE

Any unauthorized entry on premises belonging to another—whether they are homes, offices, plants, or computer centers—is trespassing. The intruder may be ejected, by reasonable force if necessary, and be either arrested or sued for any damages which he may cause. This includes destruction of property by recklessness or with malice without lawful excuse, and intent to endanger life by the damage. Making threats to damage property is also an offense in many countries.

The important fact to remember when evaluating the protection afforded by the law in such risk situations is that "property" means tangible property. It applies therefore to tangible objects, such as copies of reports, documents, magnetic tapes—but not to the information contained in these documents. Example: In a recent case in France the accused was charged with sabotage. He had intentionally erased valuable information recorded on a magnetic tape by passing it through a strong magnetic field. However, since the tape itself was undamaged the court ruled that no offense had been committed. The jury was directed to issue a verdict of "not guilty."

At common law every attempt to commit a criminal offense is itself an offense. Offenders can often be prosecuted or sued for the attempt even when it is unsuccessful. Also there remains the possibility of prosecuting villains for conspiracy when two or more persons agree to do an unlawful act, or a lawful act by unlawful means.

From the general information given in the preceding paragraphs it will be seen that some civil and criminal remedies are available to assist in the protection of businesses from the risks caused by wrongdoing, carelessness, recklessness or malice by persons inside or outside a company.

It is easy to criticize the laws in many countries for being helpless in providing relief to victims of fraud and theft, because there are gaps and loopholes in the laws which do need to be filled with new legislation. We will not, I hope, need to wait for major disasters or scandals to move the lawmakers to act.

Sometimes the law is unjustly criticized for not doing more to help victims of fraud and theft, and criticism is also leveled at police, who sometimes seem to do less than might be expected of them in investigating frauds. The fact is that most police agencies do all in their power to help, but too often their powers are inadequate.

Earlier we cited several cases of international fraud involving huge sums of money, which the villains rapidly transferred from one bank to another or in cash across international borders. Detectives investigating such cases have no power to inspect back accounts or records to aid their inquiries until sufficient evidence has been obtained from other sources for a warrant to arrest. This limitation enables many villains to escape. A judge, even if he felt positive that it was the right thing to do, could not empower a detective to examine specific bank account records as part of an investigation of fraud.

In many countries there is no provision whereby a judge can issue a warrant to search for evidence of a crime even though police have solid reason to believe that a suspect's motives are fraudulent. Very often, a properly conducted search could disclose sufficient evidence to justify an arrest before the villain had caused a substantial loss.

Another source of difficulty ·in some countries is the

lack of legislation to permit detectives to inspect the books of a sole proprietor of a business or an unincorporated partnership, although access to the books of an incorporated company is relatively easy to obtain. This fact is well known to perpetrators of big business frauds who carefully avoid victimizing corporations when "stripping of assets" is the game. They seek out one-man firms or partnerships to victimize.

UNCOOPERATIVE WITNESSES

One of the risks a company runs when it is victimized is that key witnesses may refuse to give evidence, from self-interest or some other compelling motive. As a matter of individual conscience in a free society there must be freedom to refuse to cooperate, to answer questions which are vital to the investigation of a crime. But such an attitude often delays the collection of evidence, allowing time for the villain to cover his tracks or get beyond the reach of the law. Legislation which would compel witnesses under court order to aid inquiries by answering relevant questions under oath would reduce the time now spent in many investigations of fraud and loss.

As this is being written, the investigation of a single case of suspected fraud, involving a loss of nearly $14 million to a British food products company, has taken the full time of a team of ten professional investigators. They have identified the villains but are unable to accumulate sufficient evidence to prosecute them because honest, law-abiding citizens who have no need to fear being in jeopardy refuse to be interviewed about the case. The investigation started in 1971 and may soon have to be abandoned. It is pointless to continue such expensive investigations unless the prosecution is likely to be successful, and this fact is an enormous asset to the villain.

Another problem regarding testimony and evidence

that enables wrongdoers to evade criminal responsibility crops up when the evidence is "word against word." The rules of evidence in most Western courts require the submission of evidence to prove that an offense has been committed and that there is probable cause to believe that the suspect committed the offense before they will convict. It is necessary that the prosecution submit corroboration to connect the accused with the crime. One witness whose word is disputed by the defendant, or one fact about which the defendant can give a reasonable account are not sufficient by themselves to prove a case. Very often cases of business fraud and theft hinge on "his word against mine" evidence. Since the prosecution in such cases is rarely successful, the question arises of whether it is worthwhile to institute proceedings.

A corporation lawyer in New York told me that he recently advised his client firm not to prosecute because there was insufficient corroborative evidence. An executive of a firm who frequently read documents to which he had no right was observed by his secretary. These documents were stored in the firm's computer, and he called them out by sending a coded message to the computer, which in turn displayed them on the screen of a terminal on his desk. He was suspected of using this "inside" information to guide his successful speculations in commodity markets and to cause financial injury to his employer. The secretary's statements to investigators about what she had seen were categorically denied by the executive. It was not possible to find evidence that he knew of and used the code to illegally gain access to the computer or that he had ever commanded the computer to display the documents. It was his word against that of the secretary, but the probability is that she told the truth. Tribunals rarely convict on such probabilities, unfortunately.

In such circumstances it is difficult to bring villains into line no matter how firm a stand one takes against lawlessness.

CHANGING CONDITIONS AND THE LAW

Anyone who has explored the available protections under existing laws against risks of fraud and theft becomes aware that the laws as they stand are generally inadequate. This point has been made several times in this book. Why are they inadequate?

One of the curses of our technological times is that the velocity of today's problems often seems to outdistance the ability of law makers to come up with legislation. There always seems to be a lag between the challenge and the coping with it. We are seeking protection against today's losses under laws that were written twenty-five, fifty, even a hundred years, and more, ago. This is a lag that modern industry and commerce can ill afford because the losses from wrongdoing are growing bigger. Years ago when a dishonest accountant fiddled with the books the most he could get away with would not break a company. Today, computer-aided con men have forced companies out of business.

International crime cuts so broadly across corporate and national boundaries that some people wonder if anything much can be done about it. The complexity of today's risks in security is something the business managers of the past didn't have to confront. They lived in an age when doing business was more simple. Not so long ago the owner of a business knew most of his customers personally. He saw them at the ball games, in church on Sunday, and in his place of business. Today in one-owner firms this is no longer possible. Old reliable friendly relationships between businessman and customers, employer and employees, teacher and pupils can no longer be counted on. Alienation from such human relationships has weakened the stability of our economic and business activities and our ability to tackle problems, such as the risks of loss.

When a person takes action to protect against losses he makes a change in something—a policy perhaps or a procedure or maybe a new program. Even when this action has the intended effect, it may also have other effects which are not intended. Sometimes these turn out to offset or outweigh the intended effect.

The consequences of controlling access to photocopy machines in a large German company provides an instructive example. Placing locks on office photocopy machines succeeded in limiting access to them to a few responsible employees and reduced the risk of someone making unauthorized copies of confidential documents, a process which had been costing the firm large amounts of money through information leaks. But by doing this the company also made many other employees and outsiders aware for the first time that it had information which could bring a good price from certain interested parties. Dozens of people who never in the world would have thought of stealing information and selling it started thinking about it. As a result, the incidence of leaks of confidential information increased far above the original level. Efforts to stop it seem unproductive. "As soon as people found out that we have a gold mine in our files they started to dig into it," the director of this firm told me. "Now we have a problem that is ten times greater."

"You can never do merely one thing," is the succinct way in which Garrett Hardin, a California biologist, recently expressed this profound truth about any action that changes something. It suggests that an ounce of insight is worth a pound of good intentions.

Applied to risk management, it tells us something about the people who are competent to manage loss risks. They must be tough-minded without being hard-hearted. They must not expect to find simple answers to complex risk problems and they should not have Pollyannaish notions about human behavior. They should be able to think through risk situations and, before accepting solutions, consider the predictable and the unpredictable side-effects that could result. They must be personally inspired to seek out or to develop fresh ideas for risk management. They should have the courage to recommend and implement protective measures and the vitality to sustain them.

Unfortunately, most companies would be hard put to find such talent. Competent risk managers are in short supply. Candidates for such posts are often undistinguished persons—qualified perhaps as policemen or private detectives but not to undertake to protect the life, liberty and success of a business that is continuously undergoing change in a changing world.

What is the alternative for corporations who are feeling their way among the risks in this technological age? Risks cannot be ignored. They will not go away; rather, they seem to multiply unless they are managed.

Some corporations are finding a solution to the risk management problem by drawing upon the collective wisdom and cooperative effort of all their employees— every person on the payroll.

JOB LOSS PREVENTION PROGRAMS

Because the end result of losses to a company is a cutback on personnel, a number of firms who have risk management training programs for employees focus attention on the factor most likely to motivate workers to take an active interest by labeling them "Job Loss Prevention [JLP] Programs." By learning how to apply the principles of risk management in their own areas of responsibility, employees at E. I. du Pont de Nemours— for example—are told, "The job you save may be your own."

In another multinational corporation, every employee in every facility of its widespread operations is a member of a JLP group. These groups meet once a week on company time for forty-five minutes. No group has more than twenty members, and each group is managed by a chairman, who is appointed by the office of the president of the corporation (to give weight to the importance placed on the program). The chairmen receive no special training in risk management or in leading group. All they need do is to follow the scripts and use the demonstration aids supplied to them in a training kit, called the Big Black Box.

"If the chairman keeps one jump ahead of his group in conducting the program we are satisfied," the president of this corporation told me.

The program materials included in the Big Black Box are: 26 prerecorded cassette tapes (one fifteen-minute side to be played at each session), 52 sets of illustrated flip cards, 52 outlines for group meetings, 52 guides for chairmen, 26 manuals dealing with various identified risk areas and activities, and supplies of pencils bearing reminders such as "DON'T RISK YOUR JOB—USE JLP," as well as other articles (key rings, stickers for telephones, letter openers, stick-on stamps for interoffice envelopes and company documents)—all calculated to reinforce the instruction given. In addition there are posters to be put up in the area to discourage risk taking. For example, one designed to be mounted on an employee's exit door reads: "IS WHAT YOU ARE TAKING HOME YOURS?" There are sufficient materials in each black box to keep the program going for a year, one meeting a week.

Each JLP group meeting starts with playing a cassette tape which identifies and measures one kind of risk problem. Quite often the situation is dramatized by professional actors, or it is discussed by some well known personality who is commissioned to record the script. Examples: Raymond Burr (TV's *Ironside*, and formerly Perry Mason) discusses the case of an employee who carries away company information to a new job; Mary Tyler Moore talks about risks of loss in office work; Roger Moore, the new James Bond, assesses the potential losses due to espionage; tough guy Telly Savalas, who has blown up his share of property on the screen, talks about property damage and sabotage in the business environment.

In the final moments of each tape the JLP group is presented with several questions worded so as to stimulate discussion. Then the chairman takes over for ten minutes, using the flip cards, to review the important points of risk identification and measurement. While doing this he focuses attention on particular risk areas within the everyday experience of members of his group. He then repeats the discussion questions.

For the rest of the meeting the members discuss ways and means to manage the type of risk which has been described and measured. They are encouraged to offer suggestions and the best of these are forwarded to the president of the corporation for further evaluation, and recognition by a personal letter.

An unpredictable benefit from the JLP group program in this corporation is job enrichment. Many employees welcome the opportunity to help the company solve one of its more complex problems. More important, perhaps, is that in becoming a "risk manager" the employee feels that he has acquired additional responsibility and authority. His job takes on fresh dimensions, which often gives him a sense of job freedom, although his accountability for his own work is increased. When he receives a personal letter from the president in response to his suggestions, instead of hearing nothing more about it or being told indirectly by his supervisor, he appreciates the internal recognition. The JLP group program thus brings into play motivations which enrich jobs: responsibility, personal achievement and recognition.

"Of course, we have found a certain amount of inertia among individuals in some JLP groups," the president told me. "But these are the people who pose a motivation problem in everything they do."

No employee is allowed to forget about JLP between group meetings. Neat notices, stickers and posters put up around his work area are constant reminders. A sticker on the waste paper basket he uses may read: "INFORMATION CAN FALL INTO THE HANDS OF THE WRONG PERSON— TEAR UP YOUR NOTES, PAPERS, DOCUMENTS OR DEPOSIT THEM IN THE PAPER SHREDDER." Another sticker on the telephone may say: "DOES THE PERSON YOU ARE TALKING TO HAVE A NEED AND THE RIGHT TO KNOW WHAT YOU ARE TELLING HIM?"

A given individual's attitude toward risk management is a combination of his upbringing, personality traits and the environmental, social, religious and political influences to which he has been exposed. I am sure that my attitude toward theft is quite different from that of someone brought up in the Middle East in the same generation. When I was a small boy I wanted to be a policeman because the cop on our block could steal the reddest, most mouth-watering apples from the fruit stand on the corner, while anyone else caught stealing apples would be arrested and fined. Had I been brought up in an Arab country I would have learned that the penalty for stealing even an apple is to have one hand chopped off—and I would have grown up with totally different views on risk taking.

Attitudes developed in youth do not necessarily indicate whether a person will be a good or a bad security risk as an adult in business. Statistical data on criminals show that convicted persons who were the children of ministers, judges and policemen are not uncommon. Fear of the law may be a severe deterrent to wrongdoing in later life—but it can also create more of a challenge.

Regardless of early attitudes, the conduct of adult workers is also strongly influenced by their attitudes toward their jobs. People who are discontented, frustrated and who feel they are not trusted by their employers are much more likely to do wrong than people who are working happily in a job which they believe gives them a responsibility, because it is a position of trust. As members of a JLP group they learn to respond to responsibility in a positive way.

"Our JLP group program encourages loyalty and we find that it spreads a genuine sense of security throughout the company," the president told me. "Our turnover rate in employees began to drop six months after we started the program—and it has never increased again. That's another reason why we feel that JLP is not only good for our employees it is good for business."*

*Name of firm which developed and uses this JLP Group Program withheld at their request for security reasons.

ABOUT SECURITY CONSULTANTS

Once a corporation becomes convinced that it needs risk management it may also decide that it needs experienced and trained experts who are competent to evaluate and manage the protective measures with efficiency and economy. If the corporation does not have the professional expertise in house it may go outside and hire consultants to provide these services.

Unfortunately, the majority of risk management specialists available today have nothing to offer except standard solutions in terms of alarm systems, fences, locks and safes, sophisticated security systems and guard patrols. There is no such person as a standard-type villain, and the clever villain needs to be matched by the continuing stratagems of enlightened countermeasures.

So what we find in the risk management consulting firms today are advisors having various degrees of practical or theoretical knowledge of a limited specialty. There are very few consultants who can claim to be generalists. Those experts who qualify as generalists are usually employed by large corporations and are reluctant to communicate their know-how.

As a result, good textbooks on risk management are scarce,* while symposiums and conferences on the subject are too often stereotyped presentations of warmed over maxims about security. When a generalist does speak at such meetings he seldom talks about fresh ideas and jealously guards the knowledge he has acquired.

Along with this failure to communicate the fruits of experience goes a certain amount of preoccupation with private empire-building and self-interest.

Some self-styled "consultants" are in reality security hardware salesmen who have little real appreciation of the customer's problems. A sales manual published by an

---

*One of the better ones is *Cost Effective Security* by K. G. Wright, associate editor of *Security Gazette*. Although British-oriented, it contains much universal common sense. The final section on "unquantified losses" is worth the price of the book (McGraw-Hill Book Company, New York, 1973, $12.00). A worthy companion volume is *Industrial Security Management* by T. J. Walsh and R. J. Healy (American Management Association, New York, 1971, $15.75).

international manufacturer of door locks, alarm systems and cash protection devices actually urges the salesmen of their products to commit fraud by misrepresentation when contacting customers. Each agent can purchase from the firm a silver-plated badge and identity card very similar to those carried by legitimate law enforcement officers, neatly mounted in a leather pocket case. The sales guide suggests:

> Introduce yourself as a "Crime Prevention Consultant." Never use the words *salesman* or *sales representative*. At this stage the customer does not need to know you have something to sell. Carry a clipboard with a notepad, ready to make the survey. . . . Ask about their security arrangements and write down everything they tell you. Let them do the talking. Not until they have completed their disclosures do you begin to sell. . . . Again, show the badge and ID card. This will remind them that you are a consultant. . . . Proceed to give advice. Tell them what you want them to buy, do not ask them what they want to order. They don't know, because this may be the first time they have ever seriously thought about security. They are depending on your recommendations. . . .

The technique of making a bogus "security survey" is widely used by salesmen of hardware. It is also a common practice for the "consultant" to eavesdrop on the private conversations of prospective customers to gain a bargaining advantage.

While making the survey, the consultant plants a bug (usually a wireless microphone transmitter which can be picked up on VHF [FM] channels) in the customer's office.* Once this is done, the consultant states that he

---

*We were alerted to this practice by a firm in Downey, California, which distributes a "wireless micro-mini-mike, battery operated," at under $16. "We supply two or three dozen a week to security salesmen around the country for eavesdropping on their prospects," a spokesman for the firm told me. "It is a trick used by automobile salesmen for ten years or more. I suppose we have sold 15,000 mini-mikes to salesmen and dealers in the auto industry." The units, slightly longer than a paper clip and only half-an-inch thick, are self-contained. They pick up and transmit voices without wires up to 1/3 mile through any FM radio. Federal investigators in the United States, starting late in 1973, began seizing such devices from auto dealers and other salesmen. "The equipment is used to overhear customers discussing terms among themselves after they have been left alone in a room at a dealership," states James Anderson, an assistant U.S. attorney for Maryland. "It is apparently a fairly common practice within the industry." Officials of several European auto builders (Volkswagen, Mercedes, Fiat, Peugeot) told me they have never heard of the practice but would not be surprised to find that it was going on.

must study his survey notes and prepare a report for the customer. He leaves for his own office, after making an appointment for another meeting with the customer. But he goes no further than his car, for the moment. Switching on the FM channel on his car radio, the consultant listens to the customer's conversation.

Unaware of the eavesdropping, the customers may talk frankly about how they liked the consultant, what they want to protect themselves against (break-ins by outsiders, employee pilferage, control of access to internal areas, and the like); how much they can afford to spend on security hardware, whether or not they are shopping around for security and other information that is helpful to the salesman.

Later, the consultant writes his "report of the security survey" in such a way as to overcome any "negatives" he may have heard them discussing and to recommend what they agreed between themselves in terms of risk control and costs. When he presents the report and makes his sales presentation there is a good chance that he will promptly close a sale.

During this second visit he can also retrieve his bug for use another time.

WHERE DOES THIS LEAVE THE VICTIMS?

The victims are generally people who are trying to live in a responsible manner toward other people and society in general. If they are businessmen, they try to compete vigorously but fairly and strive to develop public confidence and respect for their products or services through clean marketing practices. Economic success is, however, a prerequisite to the achievement of these aims. No business is a philanthropic institution.

"We will, with the means available to us, achieve the short-term and long-term results necessary for the prosperity of the company," says one firm's code of corporate conduct.* It is, at first glance, the kind of statement for a

*Ciba-Geigy, Switzerland.

recitation at a stockholders' meeting against the musical background of the national anthem. The tricky part is those six words "with the means available to us." In one company it could mean operating a swindle, in another merely going for the fast buck, and in a third it could mean the highest level of ethical and social conduct where the company would turn down a good investment opportunity because it would pollute the environment, or because it would take unfair advantages of an innocent person.

Which type of company runs the greatest risks of being victimized by a fraudsman or a thief? Unfortunately, it is the respectable, responsible firm. Because they try hard to play a fair game, they tend to believe that other people are more responsible than they may sometimes be. They are often the victims.

They are not the ones whose executives wake up in the middle of the night and wonder if somebody has stolen the secret on which the big upcoming deal hinges. They are not the ones who fear that when they open up for business tomorrow they will find desk drawers turned out on the floor, file cabinet locks smashed and the cash box looted. They are not the ones who think that anybody in the company would talk too much. Who, then, are they? They are the companies who fervently believe in their own sense of responsibility.

I met the chief executive officer of one such company after my talk on industrial espionage at a luncheon of the American Chamber of Commerce in the Netherlands at the Amsterdam Hilton, in May 1973.

"You are misleading people by telling them that corruption and spying are common place in commerce today. It is simply not the truth," he declared. "And this tommyrot you gave us about Mata Hari's seducing executives to obtain information. I've been in business for twenty-five years and travel all over the world. I've never even met a woman spy or had one try to seduce me to steal my company's secrets. How do you explain that?"

"Well, perhaps they do not think you have any secrets worth stealing," I told him.

"And furthermore, Mr. Farr, I do not know where you get your information about dishonest employees. Certainly not in my company. There is not a man or woman on our payroll whom I would not trust with my wallet. Every one is honest, loyal and dedicated."

I told him that he and his company were very fortunate.

Less than five months later, on the morning of October fourth, my bedside telephone rang at 3:15 A.M.

"Remember me, Mr. Farr? We talked at the Amsterdam Hilton after the AmCham luncheon last May," he began. "Listen, a terrible thing has happened. My brother-in-law, the chief engineer of our company, has disappeared. He has taken with him samples, formulae and process information for a new preparation on which the company has spent $12 million for research and pilot plant testing.

"I have it on good authority that he has sold our secrets to an Italian company that specializes in copying new products," he went on. "If I send our company jet to London to pick you up will you come to Milan in the morning and help us?"

While I felt sorry that the company suffered such a substantial loss, I cannot help feeling that the attitude of the chief executive—who really believed that "it can't happen here because everybody is perfectly wonderful"—must have reassured the villain that he could get away with his scheme.

Early in February 1974, I did visit this man when I was in Italy on other business. He invited me to come and see his new home. It was in a compound on the outskirts of Milan, surrounded by a ten-foot-high wall, with front and rear gates guarded day and night by uniformed private police, all carrying arms. There are eleven homes in this compound, all occupied by business executives. Each home has its own independent alarm system. There are even pressure-sensitive mats buried underneath the lawn surrounding the house, like land mines, so that no one can cross the grass without setting off an alarm inside the house. Everyone who enters and leaves the compound—even the milk and newspaper delivery people—are subjected to a methodical personal check. I was asked to turn out my pockets and open the parcel containing a gift bottle of Scotch I had brought. I was logged in and out. A private policeman swiftly searched my rented car with the thoroughness and skill of a customs agent. I saw a female guard standing by ready when a woman had to be searched. It was all very swift and politely done. When I left, my host gave me a copy of a book of fine art reproductions to take to my wife. And with it he handed me a pass which I had to give up to the police in order to carry the book out with me.

In less than a year this executive had swung from the extreme belief in the goodness of his fellow man to the opposite extreme of being in terror of him. And this is not an isolated case. Walled compounds, housing estates, and industrial parks are springing up throughout the Western world. There is Bixby Hill, nearby Los Angeles, where people who can afford to escape from the danger and fear of villains outside are living. It costs a minimum of $60,000 to withdraw from the world at Bixby Hill, and therefore only those who are able to afford it can escape the terror. The less fortunate must stay in the jungle outside.

There is a similar walled apartment house complex under construction between Boston and Wellesley in Massachusetts, which will have guards, guard dogs and electronic TV eyes everywhere, including inside the elevators. Security plans call for visitors to be issued passes and for residents and help to wear badges.

On Long Island, just east of Jericho, there is a new industrial park to house small companies—many of whom are engaged in secret projects—under heavy guard. Adjacent to the offices, machine shops and laboratories there is a housing development, where people who work there may live. It is possible to travel from home to work and back without ever stepping outside the perimeter fence. The place will even have a small shopping center, school, church, synagogue and theater.

R. P. Belcher, who works for one firm of architects and

planners who are specializing in this kind of construction, tells me that he knows of at least twenty similar
security developments for industrial and residential purposes that are already scheduled for completion by 1977.
One is in France, two in Germany, seven in the United
States, three in Canada, two in Mexico and one in
Japan—among others.

"I predict that we will be building walled cities within
the next twenty-five years," Belcher told me in a telephone interview from his California office.

I asked him what qualifications he has for designing
security developments.

"I've spent fifteen years in planning and building
maximum security prisons," he replied; and now he
belongs to this strange new division of the community.

Today's criminologists and penal reform experts are
urging no more prisons for the villains. But we are
building more and more prisons in the shape of walled
compounds for the honest, respectable and presumably
law-abiding citizens, at least for those who can afford to
live in them. There they can find the same security that
limited numbers of people have sought in the past for the
sake of privacy—like the estates and compounds of the
wealthy, such as the Kennedy family in Massachusetts—
and that Mafia families have built for other reasons.

All of us who are left outside can survive, perhaps, by
meeting villainy with villainy, and those inside can
likewise only survive by using villainy to prevent pene-
tration of their protected areas. Should this happen, the
decline and fall of modern civilization will be achieved
not by political confrontations or energy crises or pollu-
tion of the environment or even by ideological revolu-
tion—but by the actions of villains. Perhaps, however,
the lesson is being learned so that the tide can be turned.
The determination of the Watergate case investigators
and prosecutors not to allow more cover-ups but to let the
chips fall where they may, the introduction of new law
proposals and the sudden show of strength of judges in
imposing maximum sentences in recent convictions of

wrongdoers are hopeful signs. However, these are only glimmers of light in an otherwise gloomy picture of the world of tomorrow.

Our greatest hope for survival is that more people will be willing to hit back hard. Consider, for instance, Grandma Clara Blair, eighty-three years old, who lives in Montreal. She won a $300 bingo jackpot at a local church and she was thrilled. It was her first win ever, and she decided at once to use the money to buy an airline ticket to England to see her grandchildren for the first time in twenty-two years.

On her way home she stopped at a bar and bought a bottle of sherry with which to celebrate. She did not know that she had been followed from the church by someone who had greedy eyes on her jackpot. Grandma Blair was only a few steps from her home when he attacked her from behind. She raised her cane and hit him with it. He reeled and lunged for her a second time. His fingers grabbed at her handbag. She struck out with her bottle of sherry. He fell to the ground and curled up like a fetus to protect himself. Grandma struck him again with her cane and told him to get up. He didn't move. She poked him with her cane and she kicked him. He stayed on the pavement, whimpering; he would not stand up and face the battling grandma.

Fearing that he might run away when she went to telephone the police, Grandma Blair knocked him on the head again with her sherry bottle. This time it broke.

When a patrol car responded to her call they found her wine-soaked attacker just coming to, suffering nothing worse than a rising bump on his skull. He was hauled off to jail. Later, after conviction, a judge sentenced him to eighteen months. As for the robust and agile Grandma Blair, she boarded a jet two weeks later and flew to London for the reunion with her relatives.

Isn't it nice to know that there are people like her among us—and that they, too, can and do move faster than the villains? Also, isn't it nice that the judge gave a stiff penalty?

Once we begin to think seriously about defending ourselves against the villains around us, we are likely to be astonished at the results we can achieve. The difficulty is to get ourselves to think about self-defense in the first place.

Someone who is reading this book right now will be burgled tonight; someone else will be defrauded. Obviously we do not know who it will be, but the odds favor these things happening.

You may be the first to know.